The Magic of Angel Numbers

Meanings Behind 11:11 and Other Number Sequences, and What Your Spirit Guides Are Trying to Tell You

Layla Moon

© **Copyright 2022 - All rights reserved.**

The content contained within this book may not be reproduced, duplicated, or transmitted without direct written permission from the author or the publisher.

Under no circumstances will any blame or legal responsibility be held against the publisher, or author, for any damages, reparation, or monetary loss due to the information contained within this book, either directly or indirectly.

Legal Notice:

This book is copyright protected. It is only for personal use. You cannot amend, distribute, sell, use, quote or paraphrase any part, or the content within this book, without the consent of the author or publisher.

Disclaimer Notice:

Please note the information contained within this document is for educational and entertainment purposes only. All effort has been executed to present accurate, up to date, reliable, complete information. No warranties of any kind are declared or implied. Readers acknowledge that the author is not engaged in the rendering of legal, financial, medical, or professional advice. The content within this book has been derived from various sources. Please consult a licensed professional before attempting any techniques outlined in this book.

By reading this document, the reader agrees that under no circumstances is the author responsible for any losses, direct or indirect, that are incurred as a result of the use of the information contained within this document, including, but not limited to, errors, omissions, or inaccuracies.

Layla Moon

Table Of Contents

4 FREE Gifts	1
Introduction	6
Chapter One: Of Numerology and Angel Numbers	12
Kabbalah Numerology	13
Tamil Numerology	17
Chaldean Numerology	21
Pythagorean Numerology	26
Angel Numbers	28
Takeaway	29
Chapter Two: Angel Numbers	30
Why do we see them?	32
Types of Angel Numbers	36
The Importance of Sequence Arrangement	41

Takeaway	43

Chapter Three: Synchronicity — **44**

The Law of Divine Oneness	46
The Law of Vibration	47
The Law of Correspondence	47
The Law of Attraction	48
The Law of Inspired Action	49
The Law of Perpetual Transmutation of Energy	49
The Law of Cause and Effect	50
The Law of Compensation	50
The Law of Relativity	51
The Law of Polarity	51
The Law of Rhythm	52
The Law of Gender	53
Divine Synchronicity and Number Vibration	53
Takeaway	55

Chapter Four: Your Connection With Angel Numbers — **56**

Numerology	57
Repetitive Numbers	58
Intuition	59
Why Am I Not Seeing My Angel Number?	60
Increasing your Awareness	69

Takeaway	74
Chapter 5: Single-Digit Angel Numbers	**75**
Pythagorean Alphanumeric Cipher	76
Destiny and Life Path Number	77
Vibrations of Number 0 - 9	78
Takeaway	86
Chapter 6: Number Sequences and Combinations	**87**
Master Numbers	88
Repeating Sequences	90
Ascending Sequences	95
Descending Sequences	99
Takeaway	104
Chapter 7: Interpreting Numbers	**105**
Single Digit Virtues	106
Repeating Numbers	106
Mixed Numbers	108
Takeaway	114
Chapter 8: Angel Numbers and Manifesting	**115**
Manifesting Your Desired Reality - How To	115
Manifesting with Angel Numbers - The Basics	119
Manifesting with Angel Numbers - Rituals	122
Takeaway	125

Chapter 9: Manifesting with Specific Numbers 126

    222 Scripting Technique 128

    444 Scripting Technique 129

    555 Scripting Technique 130

    777 Scripting Method 131

    369 Scripting Technique 131

    Takeaway 138

Conclusion 139

Thank You 141

References 144

4 FREE Gifts

To help you along your spiritual journey, I've created 4 FREE bonus eBooks.

You can get instant access by signing up to my email newsletter below.

On top of the 4 free books, you will also receive weekly tips along with free book giveaways, discounts, and so much more.

All of these bonuses are 100% free with no strings attached. You don't need to provide any personal information except your email address.

To get your bonus, go to:

https://dreamlifepress.com/four-free-gifts

Or scan the QR code below

Spirit Guides for Beginners: How to Hear the Universe's Call and Communicate with Your Spirit Guide and Guardian Angels

Guided by Moon herself, inspired by her own experiences and knowledge that has been passed down by hundreds of generations for thousands of years, you'll discover everything you need to know to;

- Understanding what the call of the universe is
- How to hear and comprehend it
- Knowing who and what your spirit guides and guardian angels are
- Learning how to connect, start a conversation, and listen to your guides
- How to manifest your dreams with the help of the cosmic source
- Learning how to start living the life you want to live
- And so much more…

Law of Attraction: Manifest Your Desire

Learn how to tap into the infinite power of the universe and manifest everything you want in life.

Includes:

- Law of Attraction: Manifest Your Desire ebook
- Law of Attraction Workbook
- Cheat sheets and checklists so make sure you're on the right path

Hoodoo Book of Spells for Beginners: Easy and effective Rootwork, Conjuring, and Protection Spells for Healing and Prosperity

Harness the power of one of the greatest magics. Hoodoo is a powerful force ideal for holding negativity at bay, promoting positivity in all areas in your life, offering protection to the things you love, and ultimately taking control of your destiny.

Inside, you will discover:
- How to get started with Hoodoo in your day-to-day life
- How to use conjuration spells to manifest the life you want to live
- How casting protection spells can help you withstand the toughest of times
- Break cycles of bad luck and promote good fortune throughout your life
- Hoodoo to encourage prosperity and financial stability
- How to heal using Hoodoo magic, both short-term and long-term traumas and troubles
- Remove curses and banish pain, suffering, and negativity from your life
- And so much more…

Book of Shadows

A printable PDF to support you in your spiritual transformation.

Within the pages, you will find:
- Potion and tinctures tracking sheet
- Essential oils log pages
- Herbs log pages
- Magical rituals and spiritual body goals checklist
- Tarot reading spread sheets
- Weekly moon and planetary cycle tracker
- And so much more

Get all the resources for FREE by visiting the link below

https://dreamlifepress.com/four-free-gifts

Introduction

"All is Number."

~ Pythagoras

For as long as I can remember, I have always been fond of numbers. Well... not the complicated ones that had my head pounding after a few moments, but the more practical numbers. The numbers that help me figure out what is happening in and around my world. Even as my world was folding in on itself in high school, I spent time on Sudoku to escape it. Granted, I didn't really understand it at the time, but I always loved the feeling of solving more and more complex puzzles. As I became more enmeshed in my spiritual journey and my alignment grew, it seemed as though my love for numbers was manifesting everywhere. On one hazy day, my son and I were sick, and I was trying everything to muster enough energy to get us to the hospital. I got a random phone call from a number with 7777 in it, and it turned out to be one of my friends who took off work and drove us to the hospital. We were checked out in Room Number 7, got the hospital bill which totaled $1,776, and made it back home at 7:17 p.m. Growing up in a Christian community, I came to understand that the number 7 was connected to God, and seeing it everywhere got me curious.

When I'd somewhat recovered, I decided to see what I could find out about seeing one number that many times a day. Cue… **numerology.**

At its core, numerology seeks to understand the deeper meaning conveyed by numbers. Numerology understands that numbers have more to say about us and our lives, and it pushes us to stop and listen to the message, good or bad. When I looked into the meaning of the number 7, I was delighted to discover that there was more to it than the surface religious connotation I had grown up hearing. Number 7 denotes completion, starting over, and it is the number of perfection. Considering my condition at the time the number manifested itself so evidently in my life, I was sure this was a message aimed at giving me hope. *"Layla, you may be sick, but you are still whole. You are perfect, and you will always be okay,"* is what I heard in my heart. I was onto something! But I still had questions, questions borne of my belief in the manifestation of energy throughout our lives. Why had the universe chosen to be so blunt? What had I missed before?

Journal in hand, I called a babysitter and went into my bedroom/office to sit with myself and figure it all out. As I poured through columns, stories, articles, videos, and forums, it became clear that numerology had been playing a part in my manifestation journey, but I just hadn't paid enough attention. Falling through the cracks of my conscious mind were little nudges from the universe showing me the way to go. A lightbulb went on in my head. A month prior to the hospital visit, I had been wondering about letting my lease lapse and moving to a place I'd admired for the longest time. I knew a few people who lived in the building, so when an apartment was available, I received a few phone calls about it. But that day, the strangest things kept happening. I called the agent, who told me the apartment number, and I wrote it down. However, when I got to Apartment 606, it was still occupied. The agent didn't pick up my calls after that, and when I called the next day, the apartment had already been taken.

As I write this, I have lived in Apartment 606 for over two years. The empty apartment had been Apartment 609, which was at the end of the hall. If I had been alert that day, I'd have seen the open door and the banner propped up in the hall. When I looked through the notebook I had when I'd received the calls about the apartment, I'd written 609 six times. I'd also called the agent six times that day, five going unanswered. This is the only event I could find evidence of, but my memory churned out more instances that day. Until now, whenever I have something nagging my brain, I always find a clue through numbers - little reminders or pointers to show me what to do next. For the most part, numbers have done a great job of pulling my mind from the depths of negativity and helped me realize that the universe always has, and will always have, my back.

So, how did my afternoon locked in the bedroom go? After realizing how much I'd been missing out, I started observing more to immerse myself in my activities with greater intentionality. And this is how I realized that **Angel Numbers** were almost always everywhere.

Essentially, **Angel Numbers** are repeating sequences of numbers that offer you insight into an incident or event in your life. The messages conveyed by angel numbers can be encompassed by generalized meanings, but sometimes, the message conveyed is so particular to your situation that you cannot imagine the message is intended for anyone else. My relationship with **1111** has been long-lasting and impossible to ignore. On days when everything seems to be going according to plan, or days when changes don't faze me that much, I seem to look at my watch just as 11:11 shows. Once, I was at the gym, and my workout felt better than usual. I was having fun pushing my body to its limit, not wondering what I needed to do or my deadlines. Just as I finished a set that had me bowed over in exhaustion, I lifted my wrist to my face. The smile that split my face was almost scary. The 11:11 on the watch was absolutely magnificent to me. I was in alignment, and the universe gave me a thumbs up. I spent the rest of the day in a happy daze, and everything felt beautiful.

Moments like this have been many in my spiritual journey, and not all of them have been happy moments. I dread seeing some numbers as I am forced to sit and reexamine my thoughts, actions, and words. Sometimes I just want to sit and wallow, but this negative vibration just calls for more negativity to bombard my world, and I have to take the time to cleanse myself and my space. I have explored the beauty of spirituality for years now, and I am always amazed at the myriad of ways the universe decides to speak to us. My foray into numerology may have started as a curiosity that needed to be quenched, but now it is a practice that has been fully enmeshed in my spiritual journey, so well incorporated that I sometimes can't say for sure which practice is dominant. My soul guides me, and I rely on the universe more and more to wade my way through life.

For me, numerology is my billboard sign, the ultimate sign of manifestation. For some of my friends, it is their guide through life, a feedback tool that alerts them when they are on the right path, and when they need to adjust course. This book is my way of showing you how important numerology can be in your spiritual journey and how it can help you learn more about yourself and your world. In this book, we will explore the history of numerology, the Pythagorean cipher, and angel numbers. By exploring the different meanings of angel numbers, you will get an insight into how to interpret your angel numbers, become more open to seeing them, and incorporate them into your spiritual journey as you manifest the life of your dreams.

Join me, Layla Moon, as we delve into this beautiful world where numbers and spirituality unite to lead you into your greatest self.

Chapter One

Of Numerology and Angel Numbers

"Numerology is the bridge between who you are now and who you have the potential to be."

~ Anonymous

Claiming that one specific person invented numerology and/or angel numbers is akin to throwing out a name and saying they invented water. There is no "invention" when it comes to matters of the universe. As with many of the universe's mysteries, the history of numerology is as fascinating as it is shrouded in mystery. Not because it does not exist, but because the texts explaining its origins failed to survive the harsh effects of time. Numerology exists in different forms depending on the culture of origin. The four main categories include - Kabbalah Numerology, Tamil Numerology, Chaldean Numerology, and Pythagorean Numerology. While key factors make each of these practices unique, they are still connected, in that they employ the power of numbers to help us chart our course in life. No practice is greater than the other, and while we will focus on Pythagorean Numerology, this in no way discounts the other three. Here, I'll briefly explore the other three before we dive into our main practice.

Kabbalah Numerology

Drawn from Hebrew mysticism, Kabbalah Numerology focuses explicitly on the Hebrew alphabet, but in the modern world, this was adapted into the Roman alphabet to make it easier for some practitioners to determine their life purpose. With Kabbalah Numerology, the focus is the knowledge of the mind and soul, not our physical bodies or existence. Using our names at birth, this practice assigns us single-digit numbers that we then use to gain insight into our ideals, priorities, and motivations. Because all things exist as frequency, or energy, Kabbalah Numerology relies on our unique vibration through the energetic significance of our names to show us who we really are, and our inner purpose.

With 22 vibrations ranging from 1 to 400, the energies that form Kabbalah Numerology include:

- Kether

- Chokhmah

- Binah

- Chesed

- Geburah

- Taphareth

- Netzach

- Hod

- Yesod

- Makuth

These energies transcend the physical boundaries and limitations in the world, allowing us to understand our personalities and traits. To determine your life path number in Kabbalah Numerology, you need to assign each letter of your given name (all your names) a number. With the letter each holding a specific value, here's the decoding guide:

1 - A J S

2 - B K T

3 - C L U

4 - D M V

5 - E N W

6 - F O X

7 - G P Y

8 - H Q Z

9 - I R

With each letter decoded by its number, we acknowledge each letter's importance, significance, and value. Therefore, we are able to find the meaning embedded within part of our soul-spirit - expressed through our birth names.

> With each letter of your name decoded, add up the sum of the numbers, which will yield a double-digit, or triple in some cases.
>
> Divide this number by 9.
>
> Add 1 to the remainder, which will yield your life path number.

For example;

Layla Moon

3+1+7+3+1   4+6+6+5

    15   +   21

          36

Divided by 9, 36 yields 4 remainder 0

So, the life path number is 0+1 = 1

After decoding your life path number, use the following to interpret what it means to you;

Number 1 denotes growth and progress, and encompasses leadership and development.

Number 2 denotes harmony and cooperation, focusing on the relationships that are essential for your success.

Number 3 is the representation of creativity and expression, encompassing the optimism that often accompanies the recognition of limitless potential.

Number 4 denotes structure and practicality, a representation of limitations and stagnation.

Number 5 denotes freedom, creation, and genesis, encompassing the true nature of the adventurous spirit.

Number 6 denotes completion and fulfillment, a sense of friendship-oriented and caring nature that seeks to nurture.

Number 7 represents spiritual mysticism, encompassing magic, mystery, and spiritual enlightenment.

Number 8's cyclic karmic nature denotes achievement, success, impulsiveness, and charisma.

Number 9, the "full circle," denotes completion, a commitment to others; of selflessness and community-centric existence.

Tamil Numerology

Originating from Southern India, in the Tamil region, Tamil Numerology is mainly focused on the date of birth, and age, to reveal our nature and potentialities. Through our general and unique experience, Tamil Numerology reveals our Destiny Number, which we can use to map out our path and live according to who we truly are. Guiding us into our more profound nature, Tamil Numerology allows us to explore our life's purpose through our Psychic Number and our Destiny

Number.

> Our psychic number is drawn from our direct date of birth; *for example,* if you were born on July 27, 1991, your psychic number is 2+7 = 9.

> Our destiny number, however, is drawn from the entirety of our date of birth, as this is what determines our age. So, using the previous date, the destiny number would be 2+7+7+1+9+9+1 = 36, which is then whittled down to a single digit by addition; 3+6 = 9.

Each number carries its own unique vibration, guiding you to find out more about who you are, and your destiny:

Number 1 encompasses the energy of those who embody assertiveness and commitment. Symbolized by the Sun, those whose destinies are showcased by this number are passionately powerful and cannot be forced to do something they don't want. They make incredible leaders because of their traits, and are more than willing to indulge in lavish lifestyles.

Number 2 represents the Moon, and just like the waxing and waning cycles of the moon, those whose destinies are encompassed by this number are prone to ever-changing emotional states. However, they are also intuitive and creative people, and spiritual leanings can help them achieve emotional fortitude.

Number 3 encompasses the destiny of those who always hunger for knowledge. Symbolized by Jupiter, the destiny of 3 is encompassed in the mind and intellect, with these individuals seeking to protect their self-esteem from erosion. They are also more likely to be immersed in the classics because of their love for tradition, and they harbor great respect for their elders.

Number 4 encompasses individuals who are down to earth, which has led many to link them to Earth even though this number is symbolized by Uranus. Adventurous, energetic, pragmatic, and practical, those whose destinies are encompassed by this number are full of great ideas which they can incorporate beautifully into practice. They are prone to materialistic pursuits, but are often reliable and trustworthy.

Number 5, symbolized by Mercury, encompasses the destiny of those with a zesty spirit, who attract people to them because of their ability to lift anyone's spirits. They are highly adaptable, and love embarking on new things that challenge their skills and capabilities.

Number 6 encompasses the destinies of those who love caring for their close and loved ones, who are nurturing and compassionate. Symbolized by Venus, these individuals enjoy looking after others, although their sentimentality means that they are not inclined to be rational at times. Their empathy and compassion are unparalleled, and this is part of their charm and magnificence.

Number 7 encompasses the nature of those who are considered cold and withdrawn because of their introversion and reluctance to engage in conversation. Symbolized by Neptune, these individuals pursue the magical and mystic, and are deeply engaged in the spiritual. Despite their unapproachability, they are still sought after for advice.

Number 8 encompasses the nature of eccentric people who embody an individualistic streak that makes them quite adept at pursuing wealth and material success. Symbolized by Saturn, they have a stubborn nature, but their inherent leadership skills make them great team leaders and visionaries. Despite their goal-oriented mindset, systematic way of handling situations, and practicality, they have imaginative minds.

Number 9 is symbolized by Mars, and encompasses the destinies of those who favor a visual style, who are not afraid of delving into the deepest, darkest recesses of others' psyche to get to know people inside and out. Their spiritual nature, compassion, and sensitivity make them great people to know, but they can be so outlandish at times, and their frequency is hard to match. Because of this, finding a partner is usually difficult for them.

Chaldean Numerology

Inspired by Vedic Numerology, Chaldean Numerology is based on the belief that everything is vibration and that we need to be invested in the vibrations sent out into the universe. These vibrations are found in words, letters, numbers, events, dates, etc. Chaotic vibrations attract more chaotic vibrations, while positive vibrations attract more positive vibrations. Chaldean Numerology is believed to be highly accurate, mainly because of its focus on both names and dates. Since letters encompass specific energy, Chaldean Numerology guides us to use our current names to calculate our Destiny Number, instead of focusing on our birth names. The idea is that our current names embody our present vibrations, as opposed to our birth names, which embody our past vibrations. By changing your name, you altered your energy vibrations.

The number 9 is considered sacred in Chaldean Numerology, and is exempted from letter allocation. However, this doesn't mean Destiny and Life Path Numbers won't add up to 9. If this happens, there is still the interpretation obtained from this. The following is the Chaldean Numerology letter decoder:

1 - A I J Q Y

2 - B K R

3 - C G L S

4 - D M T

5 - E H N X

6 - U V W

7 - O Z

8 - F P

Calculating your Destiny/Expression Number, you need to add up the sum of your full name - specifically the name you use. Granted, I'd suggest using your official names instead of nicknames, as official names are the ones listed on the important documents and registered with the government.

Using Layla Moon, my Destiny Number is;

L A Y L A   M O O N

8   +   23

31

This is then reduced to a single digit; 3 + 1 = 4

In Chaldean Numerology, however, the Destiny Number is not the only one that can be derived from your name. By only adding up the value of the consonants, you obtain your

Dream/Personality Number. Similarly, adding the vowels in your name will give you your Soul Urge/Heart Desire Number. Each of these gives you a better understanding of who you are, and taking the time to ponder these meanings will give you a greater understanding of your vibrations, both good and bad. This way, you can discover any conflicting or complementary energies and work to find a center or amplify your energy accordingly.

> To calculate your Life Path Number, you need to add your date and month of birth. For example, July 27 will be calculated as; $2 + 7 + 7 = 16$, which in turn is $1 + 6 = 7$

> The Life Path Number, then, is 7.

Interpreting the messages inherent in your numbers is something personal, and you should take the time to understand the message received. As you become more comfortable with your numbers and what they communicate, you can use sub-numbers to gain more understanding and to become more in tune with your vibration, purpose, and destiny.

Number 1 encompasses the inherent leaders, those with take-charge attitudes and the ability to implement projects relatively easily. However, they can have ego issues, which is the most common trait, because of their self-centeredness.

Number 2 encompasses the creative mind, as these individuals tend to be strong creatives. They are also sensitive and compassionate, which makes them great peacemakers, although they are prone to melancholy. They may also perceive themselves as weak, which is not necessarily true.

Number 3 encompasses the Heavenly Triad - 3, 6, and 9. This is the number of growth and expansion, and individuals whose destinies lie in this number are known to be generous and growth-oriented. Their winner mentality sees them becoming a one-person army in the things they do best. However, their generosity can sometimes be a negative thing, as they can easily fall for manipulation.

Number 4 encompasses the traits of those who are methodical in what they pursue, adaptable to situations, and determined in their pursuit. They tend to think outside the box, and their commitment to their ideas can see them rebel. They love being unique, but they can sometimes be plagued by feelings of inferiority and fear.

Number 5 encompasses the destinies of free spirits, individuals who value adventure. They are also social butterflies who find it easy to relate with others. They work meticulously and harbor perfectionist tendencies, but you can't fault them for their attention to detail. However, they tend to get irritated easily, which can make them seem fickle at times.

Number 6 encompasses the destinies of those who are highly dependable, who value the stability of life. They are warm and nurturing, and are considered trustworthy. However, it's easy for them to care more about others to their own detriment, which is not great for their well-being.

Number 7 encompasses those inclined to live in their minds, as they seek knowledge and are comfortable delving deeper into the crux of things. They can be quiet and introspective, which comes across as aloofness sometimes.

Number 8 encompasses the nature of practical individuals driven by their goals, always working to achieve what they set their mind to. They make great leaders, as they can motivate others to achieve a common goal. However, their commitment and working attitude can turn them into chronic workaholics who ignore other aspects of their lives.

Number 9 is sacred in Chaldean Numerology, and is believed to be the shadow of the Number 0. While 0 represents nothing, 9 represents everything, and is thus the number of perfections. It encompasses the destinies of individuals who are genuine; who are not afraid to show exactly who they are to the world. These individuals are compassionate, generous, and honorable. However, they can quickly become over-attached to others.

Pythagorean Numerology

The foundation of modern numerology, Pythagorean Numerology is the culmination of Pythagoras of Samos' teachings about the connection between numbers and the universe. A renowned mathematician, philosopher, and metaphysician of the Sixth Century, Pythagoras believed in the mysticism of numbers, and that the entire universe could be reduced to a numerical value. Numbers, Pythagoras taught, connect us with a higher power in some way. These assertions began after he discovered that adding a series of odd numbers always resulted in a square number. The importance Pythagoras assigned to numbers is shown by the mathematical contributions he made, which are currently still used - like the Fibonacci Sequence and Pythagorean Theorem. However, at the time, Pythagoras' teachings and his school were considered cult and indoctrination, and his teachings and writings were mostly lost because of the ravages of time.

However, in the 1800s, L. Dow Balliett (Sarah Joanna Balliett) took the numerology teachings of Pythagoras and created a series of books and materials highlighting the vibrations, music, and colors of numbers. Balliett explained how numbers highlight the vibrations of one's soul; calculated through the names given at birth and changes throughout a lifetime, as well as the date of birth. The two vibrations, she explains, are a blueprint of how we need to live to attain our life's true purpose. Our soul vibrations are a message from the universe, and they are expressed in colors, music, and vibration. With each number containing its vibration and color, we are set upon this world to achieve harmony in the Trinity of Mind, Body, and Soul. Our mind and body are guided by our soul, and we cannot force or try to change our soul's vibration to fit what we want. Balliett warns that to do this will lead to a life of lack. By not achieving its purpose in one lifetime, our souls will appear in the next at a lower vibration, always seeking to ascend to the higher vibrations ascribed to the numbers 8, 9, 11, and 22. Balliett maintained that our name number vibration should either match or be higher than our birth date number. A lower vibration, she explained, is a sign of a soul that isn't aligned with the universe, and this means that we still have to work to get our vibration to match our destiny.

Balliett's teachings were a great contribution to Numerology, and I have had the pleasure of enjoying some of the texts. Granted, the writing is a little technical, but my rereads keep offering me a glimpse into new aspects of numerology every time. After Balliett, the other notable name in the history of modern numerology is Doreen Virtue.

Virtue's deep dive into numerology led to the beautiful world of

Angel Numbers.

Angel Numbers

If you look up Doreen Virtue, you'll notice that she denounced her "New Age era" and is now a staunch Christian. She calls her Angel Cards messages from demons as opposed to angels, and asks us to denounce our New Age beliefs and rely on Bible teachings. While I disagree with her about messages from demons, I respect her ability to dive into her religion with zeal and gusto, undeterred by the negative messages she's been bombarded with because of her switch. As a firm believer in manifestation, I still use Virtue's angel cards to help my manifestation journey, as they have been excellent guides in times of confusion and indecision.

Virtue's teachings highlight **Angel Numbers,** sequences of numbers that appear frequently or occasionally. These numbers, Virtue explains, have to be taken seriously when you notice them. They contain a specific message the universe is trying to convey to you; a message that will either confirm your question, or warn you about your decisions. The messages embedded within these numbers do have generalized meanings, but as you become more acquainted with your number(s), you'll start embracing the deeper meanings that are uniquely yours to interpret and embrace. TikTok has seen the explosion of Angel Numbers, but short videos are not likely to show you how magical these numbers are, and how they can place you on a path to realizing your greatest self.

This book is intended to show you this, and from the next chapter, we'll explore the intricacies of Angel Numbers and how to use them to create the life of your desires.

Takeaway

In this chapter, we've explored:

- The four main Numerology schools

- Deciphering using Kabbalah, Tamil, and Chaldean Numerology

- Key figures in the history of Modern Numerology and Angel Numbers

Chapter Two

Angel Numbers

"I could not have made it this far had there not been angels along the way."
~ Della Reese

We are constantly communicating with the universe, consciously or unconsciously. Many of us don't realize that we are doing it, which has unforeseen consequences in our realities. Growing up, I was always taught to watch how I talked and acted around others, especially my elders. I was to address everyone with respect, follow everything I was told by my elders - teachers, parents, uncles, aunties, grandparents, neighbors, you name it - and ensure that I apologized for any mistakes or harm I caused others, no matter who they were. Because sometimes I'd get smacked for my "bad" behavior, real or imagined, I lived in fear of doing anything wrong. It was better if I chose not to take a risk and maintain the status quo. "It could be worse," I told myself every time I decided not to take a chance. When my first boyfriend hit me, all I could think was, "It could be worse." And, thinking back on it, it definitely kept getting worse. I was always dealing with something negative, and it seemed like the universe was always upping the ante, finding new and improved ways to keep me in the misery loop.

At the time, I didn't know that my "It could be worse" was a message I was constantly sending to the universe, and I was getting exactly what I wanted - worse. I was stuck in a loop of my own creation, yet I wasn't taking responsibility for it. It was a two-way communication between me and the universe, and I wasn't aware of it. Much of our attention is usually on our communications and relations with other people that we don't have time to think about or explore our communication with the universe. We are always sending out messages to the universe through our thoughts, actions, and words. And the universe is ALWAYS responding. **Angel Numbers** are just the banner ads of the universe. The undeniable messages that are sent to us to guide us through life. As Doreen Virtue stated, you have to pay attention to the set or series of numbers that stand out to you. That $22.20 on your receipt, the 111 on the number plate of a car, the 22:22 on your clock, etc., all matter. And if a number pops up over and over again, you need to take time and find out what your angel is trying to communicate. If you already interpreted a message and the number is still popping up, you need to reevaluate and assess. Find out what you failed to understand and course correct.

We are living in uncharted waters, finding our way step by step. The universe is always willing to help and guide us to what we seek; the least we can do is listen. Angel numbers are the pointers on the otherwise empty map, the signs acknowledging that we're on the right path or have veered off course.

Why do we see them?

The short answer? Because we need the angels' guidance. Angel Numbers are the communication tools the universe employs when we fail to notice the subtle messages we have been receiving. The universe gets tired of speaking without our comprehension that it decides to conk us over the head, figuratively of course, with the answers we need. Have you ever been so frustrated with the lack of answers to your problem that you just followed your gut, and it turned out wonderfully? I have, a couple of times. It's a feeling like no other, a celebration of your capabilities. However, more often than not, we think it is a fluke. A one-time situation where we got lucky. But… it is not.

When our angel numbers become visible to us, it is the universe's decision to make it clear what we need to do. The same number may pop up in various situations, all in a bid to show us the way to go. Throughout my time as a numerology enthusiast and believer, I have found a pattern to when the numbers start to show up in my physical world. You may have more experience, and that's wonderful. The fact that you noticed your angel numbers means that you are in tune with the universe's communication.

- **When I'm having a great time.** I seem to always get a nudge from the universe whenever I'm having the time of my life. My life is great, generally, but it's filled with the mundane. The every day of it all sometimes leaves me feeling pretty meh, so it's always welcome when I start having fun doing something. And somehow, this is always when 11:11 pops up. Not 111, 11:11. I remember one morning, I woke up feeling groggy and somehow out of my element. I'd overslept and was frantically trying to catch up. I put music on and sat at my desk, ready to tackle the email that had piled up. I don't know how it happened, but a few minutes in, I was singing along at the top of my voice, smiling, and dancing in my seat. When I looked up at the corner of my screen, it was 11:11. I set my computer aside, turned up the volume, and danced until I was wheezing. Despite having work piled up in the morning, I was able to catch up and turn my computer off earlier than expected. I was so uncharacteristically productive that day, with none of my usual exhaustion.

This has happened to me on nights out, at the gym, and once on a particularly challenging hike. For me. 11:11 is the universe telling me to "forge forth." It's my sign to accelerate, dig deeper, and keep fighting.

- **When I can't seem to find a way forward.** I love taking on new challenges, and I believe that's why my spiritual life is as diverse as it is. I embrace the vibration of the universe and flow with the needs of my soul. However, this has led me into murky uncharted waters on so many occasions, with seemingly no way of navigating. As the frustration and confusion threaten to engulf me, on more than one occasion, the number 7 always appears in some form. I love looking for multiple 7s since they rarely occur to me, but once in a while, I find myself staring at one form of it when I am not searching. 7 has been my pickup number for a while now, the one that puts a smile on my face and reminds me why I started.

- **When life takes an unexpected turn.** I am a control freak. I love when things unfold as I expect them to, as I have planned it out in my head or planner. Despite years of experiencing the "planning fallacy," I can't stop assigning specific times to complete various goals. I push and push to fulfill the tasks within the planned times, usually forgetting to factor in my susceptibility to distraction and my tendency to get mental fatigue after a few measly hours. This is not counting my boredom streak. So, whenever something happens and throws my life out of focus, I snap. I get lost in thoughts of hopelessness before I remember that life works as it should. My energy runs wild before I can get a handle and accept my new reality. When I was saving up to buy a new car, I'd just passed the 90% mark when the bank revised my mortgage interest. I was livid; it turns out they were sending the notices to the wrong address. I only found out about the changes because the system finally updated my address correctly (I didn't buy this explanation at all!). I had to use my car savings to pay for the home as I found ways of revising my budget to reflect the new changes. When I received the new payment, it was $1811.81. I was floored.

Despite the frustrating experience, I was more than happy to pay this amount. It meant that every month, I would get a payment invoice that reflected the universe's message promoting me to approach life with a positive mindset as changes and new things unfolded in my life.

We see angel numbers because our souls are seeking answers from the universe. Because you are finally in tune with the universe, you can see the number and the intended guidance. This communication lasts as long as you maintain your connection to the universe and trust the universe's guidance to show you where you need to go. The next step you take is either shrouded in mystery or clear, depending on your trust in the universe's guidance.

However, I must mention that seeing the numbers is not the end of the story. You need to choose whether you'll accept the message and use it as intended. We are known for ignoring our gut instinct, and it is not far-fetched that we can fail to take the angel's message.

Types of Angel Numbers

Angel numbers build from single-digit to multiple-digit sequences, whose meanings are amplified when the same number repeats itself. This is akin to a megaphone, designed to get your attention no matter what. Single-digit angel numbers offer us insight into the messages we are receiving. Even within sequences, each digit is still humming its own vibration, lending its unique energy to the message to help you understand what is happening. The number 9 has a higher vibration than number 1, but this doesn't mean that it is in any way more important. The numbers come together to create the perfect sequence to portray your message, and you can't choose to ignore any number within the sequence.

Single Digits

Single-digit angel numbers offer us a glimpse into who we fundamentally are, as they are expressed in both destiny and life path numbers. Because they are the foundation upon which the sequences are built, we can always find the meaning of new sequences that appear in our lives if we are in tune with the vibration of the single digits. They come together to show us what our spirit guides want us to know. Understanding these single digits without referring to texts is a wonderful ability to add to your arsenal.

Double-Digit Sequences

Double-digit angel numbers are high-intensity messages that the universe needs us to grasp. Each digit lends its vibration to the message, amplifying it. While single-digit numbers may showcase what we need to work on, they are mostly focused on the simple matters in our lives that only need a tiny nudge to get us on the right track. With double digits, however, the universe determines that we need to work on a greater part of our life, which has a greater impact on ourselves, our situations, or our dreams. The vibrations of the numbers combine and complement each other in an undeniably powerful way.

However, double-digit numbers are often hard to spot. Because they occur everywhere, we rarely focus on them unless it is a repeating number. For example, we are much more likely to take note of 77 than 21 or 85. When it is a repeating double-digit, the universe amplifies the single digit's vibration, making it easier to spot. Also, seeing a single-digit angel number several times is not uncommon, but when we ignore it for too long, the universe deems it necessary to amplify it to make it easier for us to take it seriously. While the non-repeating double-digit sequences also occur frequently, we fail to notice them if our vibration is out of sync. Because of this, the non-repeating double-digit sequence will be further amplified, which creates the four-digit sequences we are more likely to notice if they appear a few times. Double-digit sequences give us guidance to the more complex things we experience. The answers provided by double digits come when our problems are growing more complex or when the changes we are experiencing have a greater impact on our lives.

For example, the number 2 represents cooperation and harmony

, and this may be the message the universe passes along to you when you are having a hard time handling everything on your plate. If you choose to ask for help, this may create an easier time for you. However, if you don't see this message and things get even more hectic, you may start seeing the number 22, a Master Number, which calls for you to use your creative mind to deal with your situation and find balance.

The universe will keep seeking our attention if we fail to notice the initial messages, but this doesn't allow us to slack off. Rather, it should encourage us to keep our vibration in sync with our angels so that we don't need too many reminders. This will create smooth and easy communication between ourselves and the universe, and our paths will be less bumpy.

Triple-Digit Sequences

In these sequences, three digits lend their power to the sequence to send us a message. Three-digit sequences are especially powerful because they connect us directly to the universe. They are a direct link to the cosmos and offer powerful messages that greatly impact our lives. Because of their vibrational power, three-digit sequences are easy to spot and occur more frequently. When angels communicate through three-digit sequences, you need to pay attention. Take your time to understand the message, and you will witness the immense power contained within the numbers and messages alike.

Quadruple-Digit Sequences

Quadruple-digit sequences are longer, and spotting patterns is usually very easy. They are a combination of two-digit sequences, with the power of these numbers amplified to send you the message that will create immense results in your life. My favorite number is 11:11, but I have witnessed other numbers, mostly 12:34 and 18:18. I use the 24-hour clock system, and I believe this is why my guardian angel seems to like communicating through my clocks and watches. I have a wristwatch, a few wall clocks, and desk clocks, and the counter on my skipping rope has also delivered a few surprises.

Quadruple-digit sequences are a direct communication from the angels that create life-changing moments when you start recognizing them with greater clarity. So many people don't see quadruple-digit sequences, so if you are in tune with your sequences, make sure to thank the universe for the clear message and support you are receiving. Interpreting quadruple-digit sequences may take a bit of time, and you need to learn to use this time to meditate and introspect so that you can draw the right message. If you believe you got the right message, but the sequence keeps popping up, review your choices. Work on your soul vibration; this way, you will be more in tune with the universe when you work on decoding the message.

The multiple-number sequences may seem confusing at first, but as you get used to communicating with the universe and decoding the messages you receive from your guardian angel, you'll become more comfortable with the decoding process. I have been at it for years, but I still have times when I struggle to find the right message I have received. I make mistakes sometimes, and this creates a little bit of chaos before I rectify my mistakes. This shouldn't deter you, however, as your angel numbers will still show up to give you the guidance you need whenever this happens. One thing to note, however, is that the sequence arrangement matters.

The Importance of Sequence Arrangement

Just as the numbers in the sequence each have their own vibration and inherent message, how the numbers appear is also an important factor to consider when decoding. Number 1, symbolizing new beginnings, has a high vibration, but number 9, symbolizing perfection, has an even greater vibration. The vibration rises from number 1 to number 9, and when these numbers come together, they share their power, lending the message the vibration it needs to showcase itself to you.

However, the message changes slightly depending on the way the numbers appear. Let's consider the number 1234.

When you look at your clock and see 12:34, the message is pretty clear. 1 signals new beginnings; 2 signals cooperation and harmony; 3 symbolizes good tidings are on the way; and 4 symbolizes maturity. So, 1234 generally encourages you to keep working on your goals, and you will reach your fulfillment. The number urges you to stay the course as the maturity of your actions is inevitable. However, 4321 is an encouragement to change perspective and embrace a new way of thinking as you journey into new beginnings. With 1 at the end, it signals that you will be experiencing a major change, and you need to equip yourself with the necessary tools to foster and embrace the change. The numbers are the same, but the message changes because of the arrangement.

Because of this, I urge you to find somewhere to write the numbers you notice, as you may see the same general numbers but with different arrangements. Note your interpretations at the time, and whenever the numbers pop up again later, you can compare how the messages you receive have changed over time and with the arrangement shift.

Takeaway

In this chapter, we've explored:

- Why angel numbers appear to us

- The different angel number sequences

- How the numeric arrangement of angel numbers influences the content of the message

Chapter Three

Synchronicity

"Synchronicity occurs at the intersection of your awareness, response, perspective, and action."
~ Andrea Goeglein

Have you ever received something you desperately needed at the exact right time but in a way that seemed inexplicable? When you think about that incident, nothing really seems to make sense, right? About a year back, I needed to replace my cooktop. The range I wanted was a bit extravagant, but I had eyed it for a while, and for some reason, nothing else sparked my interest. I had visited stores, browsed through countless catalogs, and obsessively looked at the cooktops in every friend's and acquaintance's house. All I wanted was to find a cheaper alternative that I liked. But no, my mind was made up. In my building, you can't replace inbuilt appliances without the owner's approval, so I sent in my request. Because my unit still had all the original appliances and upgrades had been done during the last resident's lease, the owner was supposed to replace my range at no cost. But the ones that were pre-approved were not what I wanted. In the end, we decided that I would cover the extra cost.

When I excitedly told one of my friends about it, she maintained that there was no way the owner could have overlooked such an important renovation, as he was a stickler for maintenance. My apartment was on the rent-to-own floor, and these were always getting upgrades because they had greater value. When the technician came to replace the appliances, he revealed that during the last round of renovations, one technician mistakenly replaced the appliances in the unit above mine. The mistake was only realized after I had called the owner. I knew the tenant, an avid Law of Attraction believer who'd invited me over several times for manifestation circles. Listening to that story, I felt a sort of wondrous joy take over me as I realized that my destiny had been a co-manifestation with one of my favorite people.

This is the essence of Divine Synchronicity. The universe conspires to grant your desires by means that seem, on the surface, unconnected. Divine Synchronicity is the culmination of the Universal Divine Laws at work, either through the power embedded in one law or the combined power of two or more laws. The Law of Vibration and Law of Attraction have received tremendous interest in the world, with many spiritual gurus and teachers highlighting how to work with them to create the life of our dreams, achieve happiness, and fall in love with our lives. I was drawn to the Law of Attraction long before I discovered that there were 12 Divine Universal Laws (that we know of). And the more I kept practicing, expanding, and delving deeper into my spiritual journey, the more I became aware of how the 12 Laws played a leading role in my manifestation journey. Divine Synchronicity is the outcome of the alignment of one or more laws and ourselves.

Let's explore the 12 Laws and their part in Divine Synchronicity.

The Law of Divine Oneness

This is the main law of the universe, and it highlights the interconnectedness of everything in the universe. The Law of Divine Oneness maintains that we are all connected to Source, and everything else. This means that our thoughts, actions, words, and feelings have an effect, so we need to be more deliberate with our thoughts and behavior. By growing into our true selves, we find our destiny; our way of bringing light and joy to the universe through our passions. The Law of Divine Oneness shows us that our expressions need to bring positive change, as we never know how far-reaching the consequences of our words and actions may be.

The Law of Divine Oneness is the ultimate expression of Divine Synchronicity, as it is the thread that links everything in the universe.

The Law of Vibration

If you have practiced the Law of Attraction or studied Numerology to any extent, then you are already familiar with the term *Vibration*. The Law of Vibration, also known as the Law of Energy, states that every single thing in the universe is in constant motion. However, the level of vibration differs, with manifestation occurring when our vibration aligns with the vibration of what we seek. Divine Synchronicity is the alignment of vibration, fostering the manifestation of the desired outcome.

The Law of Correspondence

To quote the legendary Egyptian sage, Hermes Trismegistus, "As above, so below, as within, so without, as the universe, so the soul...."

The Law of Correspondence states that the state of your physical world results from your internal state. Your internal world is reflected in your reality. If your reality is filled with lack, check your thoughts and sentiments. Your thoughts may be filled with content related to lack or inadequacy, which becomes your state of being. Your internal world needs to reflect abundance before you experience it in your reality.

The Law of Attraction

Like attracts like. This is the basic foundation of the Law of Attraction. This is the most popular Universal Divine Law, and it has received extensive coverage from believers and critics alike. According to this law, you attract what you focus on, making you the creator of your own reality. If your focus is on the things you don't want, that is precisely what you will get. Therefore, your focus should be on what YOU WANT. The Law of Attraction calls for you to believe in what you want to manifest, as doubt will lower your vibration. Your belief is the fuel that will propel the engine of manifestation, and you need to have irrevocable faith in the Universe's ability to make your dream a reality.

The Law of Inspired Action

Aligning your vibration with what you want is just a part of the manifestation equation. The Law of Inspired Action highlights the actions we take based on the inspiration we receive from the universe to guide us closer to our manifestation. This is the physical aspect of manifestation, which complements our internal work to raise our vibration into alignment with our desires. As Vasavi Kumar, a social worker, puts it: "Inspired action is that gentle, internal nudge. It's not always a plan of action."

The Law of Perpetual Transmutation of Energy

The Law of Perpetual Transmutation of Energy maintains that energy is constantly in flux, and this means that you have the power to change your vibration. Higher vibration can consume and influence lower vibration, which for us, is great news. This law reiterates our own control over our own energy, meaning that we can take steps to raise our vibration instead of wallowing in lower vibrations and manifesting a reality we don't want.

The Law of Cause and Effect

This law maintains that our action always elicits a reaction, even if the response is not immediate or noticeable. Also known as the Law of Karma, this law highlights how our thoughts and internal state, in turn, affect our reality and influence the experiences we have. Attempting to fix the external reality without first working on our thoughts and vibration is pointless because we cannot change the effect without first changing the cause.

This law also calls us to choose our thoughts and actions wisely because they will ultimately come back to us, time notwithstanding.

The Law of Compensation

The Law of Compensation states that we get what we give. It is essentially "You reap what you sow." This law, like the Law of Cause and Effect, highlights our power in dictating what happens in our life. It is about being mindful of what you put into the universe and choosing to give positivity, as this is what you will reap. Essentially, what you give is what you get.

The Law of Relativity

We are constantly comparing our lives with others, feeling better when we think we are much better off, and catastrophizing when we feel like we are losing, especially compared to people we know. Social media has worsened the comparison game, creating a world where we think things have to go a certain way for us to be "happy" or "successful." However, the Law of Relativity highlights that how we interpret our realities is rooted in our perception. The world is neutral, and we are the ones who assign meaning to it from our own perceptions. That's why two people may experience exactly the same thing but draw wildly varying conclusions.

The Law of Relativity reminds you that the world is neutral, and that you need to prioritize your own peace instead of fighting to show your "truth." It's all relative anyway, so why not work on creating the reality you want?

The Law of Polarity

Everything in the universe has its opposite. This is the basic tenet of the Law of Polarity. Where there's good, there's bad. Where there's darkness, there's light. Just because you see one side does not negate the existence of its opposite. This law reminds us that for everything we don't want, there's something we do want. So, if nothing else, always focus on what you want, even when you are facing adversity. This way, you remain rooted in what you want, leading to its manifestation.

The Law of Rhythm

The Law of Rhythm, also known as the Law of Perpetual Motion, highlights that everything is subject to cycles. The four seasons, the human growth cycle, are part of this perpetual motion. This law calls for us to embrace the cycles, to go with the flow instead of fighting against them. No cycle lasts forever, so even if we are caught in a period of pain and misfortune, we need to ride the wave, to work with it until we come out the other side.

This doesn't mean giving up, but rather, giving yourself the opportunity to gather the strength to make it through. For example, if you manifest what you don't want, the solution is not to assign blame or deny your situation. Rather, you need to accept your situation and work on changing your focus.

The Law of Gender

The Law of Gender highlights the energy inherent in the feminine and masculine archetypes, the yin and yang (or anima and animus). The feminine energy embodies creativity, intuition, spirituality, and emotion, while the masculine energy embodies logic, action, objectivity, and confidence. The Law of Gender maintains that to live by your true self, you need to balance both energies. Society favors the masculine energy, but focusing on this alone will leave you drained and off balance. You need to embrace both energies to live in alignment with your authentic self.

The 12 Divine Universal Laws govern our daily lives, and our alignment with them creates a life of vibrational and manifestation abundance. When we understand and embrace these laws, our authentic selves find a way to shine through, and this vibrational abundance means that we are in alignment more often than not. Divine Synchronicity, therefore, becomes a staple in your existence, guiding you through every step, no matter how small or big.

Divine Synchronicity and Number Vibration

Angel numbers are the physical manifestation of Divine

Synchronicity, the evidence of your vibrational alignment - governed by the Divine Laws. As your vibration increases to match your desired outcome, the universe matches this vibration with signs of its own, which at the time, usually seem like a bunch of fortunate coincidences. These coincidences are Divine Synchronicity in play, which may span a short time or stretch out for years. When you start noticing your Angel Numbers, you need to express gratitude to the universe for the sign you've received. Angel Numbers are the most common sign of Divine Synchronicity, and as your vibration keeps rising, so does the frequency of these sightings.

Embrace the universe's message, and remember that you cannot force the universe to show you its signs. Divine Synchronicity works with your choice to let go of your egoist mind and surrender to the universe, believing in the universe's ability to lead you to your true self and your destiny. So, don't watch your clock like a hawk for 11:11, and don't try to manipulate your purchases to get the desired number on your receipt. This has nothing to do with Divine Synchronicity, as you are trying to direct the universe, and this is impossible.

Angel Numbers, like their constituent single digits, have their own unique vibration, which makes them visible to us when we are ready. Our alignment to the number(s)' vibration, and our belief in the universe's ability to show us the right way, creates the perfect situation for the number(s)' physical appearance. So, the key to seeing your Angel Numbers is by working on your own vibration, allowing yourself to reach the right state to receive your destined message.

Takeaway

In this chapter, we've explored:

- The 12 Divine Universal Laws

- The connection between Divine Synchronicity and the Divine Universal Laws

- The connection between Divine Synchronicity and the vibration of Angel Numbers

CHAPTER FOUR

Your Connection With Angel Numbers

"You cannot perceive what you are not in the vibration of."
~ Darryl Anka

When you start noticing Angel Numbers, it's hard for you to go back to not seeing them anymore. However, some people have never "consciously" seen their angel numbers. I say consciously because the numbers may have been appearing, but because it is not so frequent or not the same number each time, they fail to recognize them even if they wish they saw them. My angel number is predominantly 1111, which I see pretty much all the time, with a few exceptions. However, because angel numbers are just as diverse as we are, you may fail to notice them because they are not talked about as much, or you have no idea what **your** angel number is. Finding your angel number is relatively simple, though, and here are the two main ways you can do it:

Numerology

Numerology can seem a bit complicated because of all the sub-numbers that can be created, but finding your angel number is easy because you just need to use your birth date. Just add the digits of your date, month, and year of birth, reduce it to a single digit, and… voila!

Let's say you were born on May 25, 1996. Your Angel Number, in this case, would be:

5 + 2 + 5 + 1 + 9 + 9 + 6 = 37

Because this is a double-digit, you need to add the digits again until you get a single digit:

3 + 7 = 10

1 + 0 = 1

In this case, your Angel Number is 1.

We'll explore the interpretations of these numbers, so for now, just take note of your number. However, if your total is 11, 22, or 33, you don't need to reduce them because they are **Master Numbers.** We'll explore the meanings and interpretations of Master Numbers later, so watch out for that. Or, if you're curious, skip ahead and then come back once you've satisfied your curiosity.

Repetitive Numbers

These numbers may or may not be connected to the number you got through numerology. This is how I found my angel number, and I know many people who got their angel number this way. In this method (I use this word for lack of a better one), you need to raise your vibration to become more aligned with the universe, and ask your angel to show you your number. Don't try to force it, but become more aware of the physical world around you and pay attention to numbers that seem to jump out at you. If a sequence of numbers appears frequently, or you notice it on different occasions, pay more attention to it. This may be your angel number.

If the sequence keeps reappearing, monitor what is happening in your life when you see the number. Throughout this time, keep your vibration up by journaling, expressing gratitude, and meditating. Never try to force the universe's hand, as this never works. By doing your part and letting the universe work in its own time, you will soon see the message you were looking for. Your angel will always grant your wish as long as you remain connected to Source and send out a positive vibration.

These are the two main ways to find your angel number, but there is a third one, which requires tremendous patience, and is somewhat a combination of the other two:

Intuition

This may seem pretty self-explanatory, but the process is not really straightforward, as it requires tremendous input from you. This method (for lack of a better word) calls for you to remain in tune with Source and your emotions. You already know your angel number, calculated by numerology, and you will watch out for its appearance. However, you also need to monitor your interaction with other numbers through constant journaling. As you meditate, you need to be aware of any numbers that appear in your mind, and as you make your way through the day, note the times when you feel a substantial shift in your emotion, especially leaning towards the positive.

There was a long time when I wasn't seeing my angel number, and my numerology number, 9, also seemed elusive. So I set out to figure out what was going on, and after weeks of doing everything to keep my vibration high, I finally realized what I was missing. For some reason, I kept losing sleep at 3:33 a.m. multiple times a week, or I would need to use the bathroom at that time. But I never noticed this until I put a digital table clock on my bedside table. My Angel Number had shifted, but because I'd been too wrapped up looking for 1111 or 9, I didn't notice how my emotions would shift whenever the number 3 appeared in my life. Keeping tabs on my vibration and emotional shifts finally gave me a chance to find out what I was missing. And once I saw 3:33 on my clock after I'd placed it in my room, a sense of peace washed over me. I had found my angel's message.

So, don't box yourself in as you search for your angel number. You need to trust the universe and let go of any tight hold you may have about seeing your angel number. It will appear when the time is right, and you need to be ready and open to receiving it.

In the meantime, however, let's explore some of the reasons why you may not be seeing your Angel Number.

Why Am I Not Seeing My Angel Number?

Your angel number kept appearing all the time, and suddenly you can't see it anymore. Or you've never seen your angel number even though you've been manifesting your dream and sending positive vibrations into the universe. This must mean that something is wrong, right? Not necessarily. The reason why we never see, or stop seeing, our angel numbers vary, and it's not always bad news when you don't see them. Some circumstances do call for deeper reflection and changes to be implemented, but this is not always the case. Not seeing angel numbers is actually good news sometimes.

Some of the most common reasons why we stop seeing, or don't see, our angel numbers include:

It's already manifested

Angel Numbers can stop appearing when your manifestation is complete. The universe has already granted you your desire, and since your wish is fulfilled, there is no more need for further guidance until you reach for something new, or shift direction. Angel Numbers are usually there to guide us or affirm our choices, and once we've completed the journey to manifestation, the universe gives us time to enjoy the manifested desire.

During this time, you get to revel in the fruits of your journey, take a moment to feel the magnificence of your manifestation, and express gratitude to your angel for this successful guidance. In this instance, not seeing angel numbers is a great thing, and you need to be grateful for this instead of panicking and losing faith in Source.

Your guidance has already been provided

Other times, Angel Numbers stop appearing because we have already received guidance. The manifestation is not yet complete in this case, but your angel has already delivered the message, and they are waiting for you to take action based on the guidance. I have found that when this happens, it's mostly because we have interpreted the guidance wrongly, and our angel is waiting for us to realize our mistake and course correct.

If your manifestation is not complete, think back to the last time you saw your angel number, and reflect on your actions after. Is there any path you could have taken but ignored? Did you follow or ignore your intuition? How did you feel about the action you took based on your interpretation at the time? Could there have been a different message within the number? By reviewing your actions, you monitor what happened after, and this will help you find the right message.

However, sometimes we may have received the message but failed to implement it because of fear, or we're waiting on the "right" time. If this is the case, your angel is patiently waiting for you before sending you a new message.

Your focus may have shifted

Even though the goal of our journey is to connect with who we truly are, this path is not direct. The circumstances in our lives change, and our focus shifts to accommodate this new information. As I was gearing up to start writing the first time, I was sure I had everything I needed. However, my son decided this was the right to pick a new hobby, and I needed to be more involved since classes were about 40 minutes from our home. My usually open evenings and weekends were now taken up by the commute, and I had to start picking him up from school in the afternoons to drive him to practice. I sat with him as he went through his lessons, working out what he needed and the support I could give him to allow him to pursue this. This meant I had to postpone my work, which I usually did in the afternoon, and push it to late nights. My focus had shifted to my son, and I had to take a break from my writing stuff. Sometimes these changes are bigger, and more consuming. It may be a lost job, a transfer, the death of a loved one, or just a general internal shift that guides you in a different direction. When this happens, the universe begins conspiring to help you through your new journey.

In response, your angel may take a step back just to observe how you are faring on this new path, waiting for the moment you will ask for guidance or be open to receiving one. As you become more immersed in this new path, your angel will start sending you what you need to manifest your new desires. All you need to do is keep your faith in the universe as strong as ever, and keep your vibration in tune with Source.

You're being impatient

The universe does have moments when it provides answers almost immediately, but this is not always the case. The universe's timing is always right, and trying to push for an answer because you feel like too much time has passed won't produce an answer. Instead, this will cast a vibration of doubt, and your requests will lose the momentum they had gained when you trusted the universe to give you an answer. Your angel numbers will appear when the time is right, and you are not the one to decide what that right time is. You are a co-creator, meaning you have your part to play, which is what you need to focus on. The universe will work using the momentum of your vibration, and impatience lowers your vibration, as it's almost always accompanied by doubt.

If you feel like you need to have an answer now, take a step back. Find your way back to trusting the universe completely and implicitly, and focus on sending out positive vibrations and finding alignment with Source Energy. Before you know it, your answers will present themselves. Letting go of the need for immediate answers is an important part of manifesting your angel numbers.

You're not in alignment with the universe

The Law of Vibration is one of the most important laws in manifesting, including manifesting angel numbers. Communication with the universe, Source, and our angels is possible because of the alignment of our vibration with that of the universe. Let's use the analogy of a radio station. To listen to the station you want, you have to set the frequency to match that of the radio station. This is the same with walkie-talkies. Your vibrational frequency is important if you want to receive feedback from the universe.

If you are no longer seeing your Angel Numbers, your connection may have been lost because you are no longer aligned with your angel. As previously mentioned, you need to focus on increasing your vibration to the right frequency so you can see the numbers your angel has sent to you. Meditation, gratitude, affirmations, journaling, etc., are all activities you can indulge in to raise your vibration and find your alignment again.

You're focusing on the wrong signs

I am sure you know this, but I'll write it out just in case my assumption is flawed. The universe communicates in many different ways, and angel numbers are just **one** communication tool. So, you may be looking for angel numbers when the universe has sent your message in a dream, through an unlikely helping hand, or through fortunate coincidences that seem to always teach you a lesson. Over the past few weeks, my productivity has been falling, and my sleep schedule has suffered because, by the time I've mustered enough energy to work, it's already too late into the night. But for the past two weeks, the universe has been filling my brain with motivational content through unlikely means. When I listen to a song, I usually just bop to the tune or belt out the lyrics, never thinking much about it. Recently, however, I've been looking past the music, thinking about how the singer took time to get to the recording studio, singing over and over again until they got it right. I have imagined how actors have to wake up early or fail to sleep just to get the scenes shot in time. I have been thinking of all the artists who draw and illustrate the manga (Japanese comic books) I love, the authors who took a risk and let it all out on page.

The culmination of it all was the night that I couldn't sleep and randomly decided to watch an episode of an anime I have been watching when the mood strikes. The episode just happened to show the protagonist struggling to create their artwork because of the constant stress they'd been under, and finally finding the answer at a seemingly inopportune time, the very last minute. I still don't know if he made it because I haven't watched the last episode. For me, this was the universe's message of encouragement, and it worked! I love music, animations, and manga, and all my messages were delivered through these media.

So, if you are not seeing numbers, could there be something else you're ignoring? There may be signs all around you, but your focus is only on numbers. I know this book specifically focuses on angel numbers, but this should not deter you from ensuring that your message is not elsewhere. Allow your vibration to guide you to the right sign.

You're asking the wrong questions

Another reason you may not be seeing your angel numbers anymore may be because you are seeking guidance on the wrong thing. How is this different from being on a different path? Well, when you seek guidance, your angel understands the most important aspect of your journey and sees beyond your emotions or struggles at the time. Imagine you are frustrated at work because of the workload and your colleagues' reluctance to help. But, you have not asked for help; rather, you just complain about your workload, hoping someone takes that as a hint to offer help. As your frustration grows, you turn to the universe to help you find a new job. But this is not what you need to focus on, is it? You have not really asked for help, and by constantly complaining about the workload, your focus is on it, and you attract more of it. In this situation, your focus should be on gaining the courage to ask for help or to talk to your supervisor about the workload.

This is sometimes what happens when we turn to the universe for help. We fail to look past the surface-level issues and ask for guidance on the wrong thing. And until we look deeper and find the root cause, our angel can't guide us because it will lead us astray. This is why you need to meditate and introspect before seeking guidance. Your emotions at the moment can also cloud your ability to see the situation clearly, and you should always hold off asking for guidance until you gain clarity.

You are receiving a new guardian

In some cases, the direction of your path may be such that your guardian angel feels ill-equipped to sufficiently guide you, so they call upon the power of greater angels or an angel who understands your situation much better. This does not mean that your angel has abandoned you; rather, they have guided you to the end of your journey with them. When this happens, you are more likely to start noticing new numbers, usually ones with a higher vibration than the previous ones.

This change in guardians may be permanent, which means your vibration has reached a new high, or it may be temporary. The new guardian may just be there to get you through an especially treacherous path before you get back on track, and back to your usual guardian. Whichever the case, losing sight of your numbers will always be followed by greater manifestations and an explosion of numbers in your life.

Increasing your Awareness

Because your vibration is the key to alignment with the universe and your angel, you need to work on raising your vibration to be in a better position to see your angel numbers. In this situation, noticing your angel numbers is the manifestation you seek, which will guide you on your path to your ultimate manifestation.

To raise your vibration, here are a few activities you can indulge in. Please note that this list is by no means exhaustive, and the key is to do the activities in a way you enjoy, not as an obligation. This would be counterproductive.

- **Self-care:** Self-care is as diverse as we humans are diverse, and there's no "right" way of undertaking it. The point of self-care is to leave you feeling content, rejuvenated, and at peace. By adopting practices that leave you feeling better emotionally, physically, and psychologically, your vibration will increase.

- **Affirmations:** Affirmations are simple, concise, and positive statements we repeat to ourselves to affirm our desired manifestations. Affirmations can help us overcome pervasive negative thoughts that lower our vibration, and speed up our manifestation. However, you need to believe in the affirmation you are uttering, as doubt will skew the energy you send into the universe.

- **Meditation:** Meditation is a great way of slowing down the momentum of negative and/or pervasive thoughts, as it gives you a chance to step away from yourself and observe your thoughts. Through self or guided meditation, you can clean out your mind and adopt the positive thoughts that will amp your vibration.

- **Yoga/Exercise:** By subjecting your body to the challenges of exercise, you are always left feeling better. Whether it's through yoga, dance, weightlifting, or a brisk walk, there is a feeling of euphoria that accompanies these activities, and you can use this to charge your vibration. Exercise takes you out of your mind for a while, and by using this time to focus on positive thoughts, your vibration will be substantially higher than when you started. However, you need to always stay on guard because you may find yourself ruminating once exhaustion hits. When this happens, recite affirmations that you know always leave you feeling better.

- **Music:** I love music, and this is usually my go-to whenever I feel like my vibration is slipping. My mind is prone to ruminating, especially about the wrongs I commit against others, even if it was unintentional. So, whenever I am having a hard time, I always doubt my abilities, and my mind starts reminding me why I deserve to be going through hard times. Silencing this voice can take a while, so I learned to put on a playlist to match the mood. It doesn't matter how far down the rabbit hole I went. The music always draws me out. I find myself focusing on the familiar lyrics instead. And I am not the only one whose vibration is raised by music. Music is one of the fastest ways to come out of a funk, even as you recite your affirmations. If you can, create a playlist that you know works wonders just in case you won't have time to search for a song when you're in dire need of a boost.

Watching your favorite movie or reading your favorite quote or book is also a great substitute if music isn't for you. As long as the content you consume is positive and puts you in a better mood, indulge in it to raise your vibration.

- **Journaling:** Journaling is a versatile practice that you can adopt to any situation, and it will leave you feeling slightly better than when you started. If your mind is overflowing with worry, doubt, or negativity, writing it all gives you a much-needed outlet, and you can use the journal to highlight arguments countering your doubts and worries. A gratitude journal is also a great way to raise your vibration, as it forces your mind to find the good in your life, no matter how small. A journal recounting the day's events keeps your mind clear, and you can plan your next course of action through it. No matter how you choose to undertake this practice, journaling allows you to take a deeper dive, which is usually impossible if you're stuck in a loop of thoughts. With a clearer mind, you have a higher chance of raising your vibration by replacing worrying thoughts with more positive, empowering ones.

- **Gratitude:** Taking the time to express gratitude for the things you have or who you are, is a great way to boost your vibration. Appreciating what you have sends a powerful message to the universe that shows your readiness to receive even more of what you want. Gratitude puts us at a higher vibration because we are reminded that we have a lot of good in our lives, no matter how small they may be. A daily gratitude practice is the perfect way to keep your vibration high, and on days you may find it difficult to find the good in your life, perusing through your journal will help remind you of all the good that has been part of your life.

- **Acts of Kindness/Service:** Sometimes, the key to breaking our own negative loop is stepping away from ourselves completely and focusing on others. By taking the time to make someone else's day or time marginally better, you are bound to feel much better yourself. This may seem selfish, but it really is not. Acts of kindness are mutually beneficial, and finding a moment to indulge in something for someone else can help us find our smile.

It's worth saying that even as you raise your vibration, you need to remain patient and let the universe work in its own time. Enjoy the process and let go of your need to see your angel numbers. You will find more ways of communicating with the universe until the numbers make their way to you again. Don't lose hope, and don't be tempted to make these activities an obligation just so that you can see the numbers. The universe appreciates genuineness, and disingenuity will move you further and further away from your goal.

Takeaway

In this chapter, we've explored:

- How to find your Angel Number

- The reasons why you haven't seen, or stopped seeing, your Angel Number

- What to do to raise your vibration and increase your chances of seeing your Angel Number

Chapter 5

Single-Digit Angel Numbers

"If even God is referred to by using the number, why don't you think that your birthdate and numerical values of the letters that build your name up are also telling you something?"

~ Zainurrahman

In Chapter One, we explored the history of modern numerology, Pythagorean Numerology. In this chapter, we'll dive deeper into how we can use numerology to interpret the messages we receive through our Angel Numbers, starting with the foundational numbers - single-digit numbers. To better understand why numerology is important, we'll use the Pythagorean alphanumeric cipher to see how our names and date of birth greatly contribute to how we interpret the numbers we receive from the universe.

Pythagorean Alphanumeric Cipher

The Pythagorean alphanumeric cipher is an important tool in numerology as it allows us to find the root of our names, the number that guides us to our destiny. With the cipher, you get to find your Destiny or Expression number, which guides what you need to do to align with your life's purpose, expressed through your Life Path number.

Our Destiny and Life Path numbers each have their vibration, and when we are in alignment, our lives feel content and peaceful. To determine your Destiny number, all you need to do is convert each letter of your full name (the official name listed in your official documents) to its root number using the cipher and add up the digits until you reduce it to a single number or a Master Number.

Please use the cipher below to calculate your Destiny Number.

1 - A, J, S

2 - B, K, T

3 - C, L, U

4 - D, M, V

5 - E, N, W

6 - F, O, X

7 - G, P, Y

8 - H, Q, Z

9 - I, R

Destiny and Life Path Number

Using Layla Moon, my **Destiny Number** is;

LAYLA		MOON
3+1+7+3+1		4+6+6+5
15	+	21
	36	

This is then reduced to a single digit; 3 + 6 = 9

To calculate your **Life Path Number**, you need to add your date and month of birth.

Reusing the example provided in Chapter One, July 27

will be calculated as; 2 + 7 + 7 = 16, which in turn is 1 + 6 = 7

Your Life Path Number shows you your life's purpose, or goal. It is the expression of your soul's vibration, and shows you what you need to aim for in your life to find your true self. This is your life's greater goal, and your Destiny Number is the vehicle you will use to get there. Your Destiny Number, also known as Expression Number, highlights your strengths and weaknesses, calling for you to capitalize on your strengths to achieve your life's mission. Because it also points to your weaknesses, your Destiny Number is also a representation of things you need to work on so that they do not hinder your progress towards aligning with your true self and achieving your destiny.

Let's look at the meaning of each number so you can discover who you are and life's purpose.

Vibrations of Number 0 - 9

As highlighted in this book numerous times, each number holds its own unique vibration and meaning. When we explore the interpretations of single digits, we highlight the fundamental vibration of angel numbers. By understanding the vibration of each number, you understand your Life Path Number and

Destiny Number, as well as the angel numbers that serve you on your path. This understanding will also help you to gain greater clarity when the angel numbers you encounter have no generalized meaning.

Zero

0 is the representation of infinite, and nothingness. It is the number used to symbolize Source, or as the ancients put it, "God Force." When it appears with other numbers, zero becomes an amplifier, magnifying the vibration of the other numbers.

The number zero calls for us to listen to our higher self and to move beyond the limitations of this world. It signifies the beginning of a spiritual journey and highlights the uncertainties that are part and parcel of this new journey. Your Life Path Number and Destiny Number will never add up to zero, because their vibration serves to bring us closer to Source.

One

Number 1 symbolizes new beginnings, creation, and autonomy. 1 will exhibit out-of-this-world ambition and willpower, and their drive is unmatched. The goal is to forge forward and achieve what needs to be done, and 1s make great leaders. However, they can also be stubborn, and their willpower can quickly become arrogance and inflated self-importance. For 1s, the need to be self-sufficient drives them, but if the negative traits are not checked, they can quickly push people away.

Number 1 usually appears when we are about to embark on something new or when our path is changing. It is usually a sign of encouragement from the universe, as this may mean that we must find the courage to face new challenges, or relax and enjoy the new manifestation.

Two

Number 2 is linked to sensitivity and harmony, with 2s having the innate ability to sense energy and emotional shifts. Because they thrive in harmony, 2s always draw on their compassion and empathy to bring harmony in relationships and situations. However, they are conflict-averse, and may choose to suffer in silence to avoid sparking conflict, or they may bow to the will of others to avoid conflict. 2s have to be careful about relying too much on external validation, and they have to work to rise above their fear of the unknown and fear of unplanned change if they seek to avoid stagnation.

When we see Number 2, the universe calls for us to lean on our strength to keep moving forward. It can also be a call to accept help if you are struggling, but to be careful not to let the other person derail your path. Number 2 essentially highlights the importance of harmonious cooperation, but warns against losing ourselves to the will of others.

Three

Number 3 is linked to creativity and self-expression. 3s are known to value communication, and their expression flows through various media, including writing, art, and music. They enjoy sharing, and this joy is amplified when they make others smile. Number 3s are social, adventurous, and spontaneous, traits that make them popular with others. However, they have mood swings that can be extreme, bordering on mania, which can make people wary of them. 3s are also prone to withdrawing emotionally when they feel misunderstood, and they can adopt indifference as a coping mechanism to avoid the pain of rejection.

When the number 3 appears, it is a sign from the universe that good things are coming your way. 3 is a reminder from your angel to remain positive, have faith in yourself, and remain steadfast even as challenges plague you. Number 3 is a sign of optimism.

Four

Number 4 is linked to discipline and structure, and 4s thrive in structured systems. 4s are practical and hard workers, as they need to achieve stability. They will approach situations conscientiously, with the seriousness they deserve, and are highly dependable. However, this need for structure and order can result in rigidity and an inability to adapt. If not checked, this can lead to needless suffering because life is constantly changing, and adaptability shows trust in the universe to lead you to your goal.

When we see the number 4, it is a message from the universe that we have the love and support of our guardian angel. It is encouragement from the universe to believe in ourselves and take risks, as change is inevitable.

Five

Number 5 is linked to freedom, and 5s are adventurous spirits who move at the beat of their own drum. They are courageous and brave, and they find life lessons in their acts of bravery. Their spontaneity keeps life interesting, but on the flip side, they can be rash and restless. Others may find them irresponsible and reliable, and their noncommittal nature may prevent some from giving them a chance. 5s can benefit from creating a structure that allows them the time and space to indulge their spirit.

The appearance of the number 5 is a sign from the universe that big changes are coming, and you need to be prepared for this period of personal growth. Change is never easy, and the universe is giving you a warning AND encouraging you, so you need to be prepared to rise above whatever comes your way.

Six

The belief that number 6 is an omen has permeated societal beliefs so much that many people shy from this number. This cannot be further from the truth. 6 is the number of domesticity, home, and family. 6s are known as nurturing souls who are empathetic and supportive. They love taking care of their family and close friends, and revel in the stability of a well-tended-to home. However, this care and concern they express can become overbearing. Because they are caretakers, they may believe that they are better than others because of their selflessness, and this superiority complex may be counterintuitive. They are also prone to stress and can become submissive to the point of neglecting themselves to serve others. 6s can benefit from finding a balance, a way to ensure that they *and* others are taken care of.

The appearance of number 6 is usually a message from the universe prompting us to evaluate our lives. It is a call to connect with the spiritual, even in our pursuit of the material. Our guardian is sending a sign that we need to find balance in our lives through connection with the divine, ourselves, and others.

Seven

Number 7 is linked to spiritual awakening and enlightenment. Number 7s are introspective beings who tend to think a lot. Their analytical skills are top-notch, and they tend to be drawn to the mythical and spiritual. If they are not careful, 7s can easily be sucked into a loop of hypercritical and pessimistic thoughts. They are also prone to resentment, and they don't like compromising. 7s can also be self-righteous, especially if they make incredible progress in their spiritual journey.

The appearance of number 7 is an assurance from the universe that divine powers are at play, and that you need to trust yourself to overcome the hurdles that will appear in your way.

Eight

Number 8 is linked to abundance, material wealth, and financial success. 8s are known for their relentless ambition and goal-oriented focus, which sees them scale to leadership positions with seemingly relative ease. They are self-assured, self-confident, and self-reliant, with their strength assuring those around them that they can attain their goals. Because of their tenacity and single-minded focus on the goal, 8s can develop a superiority complex and be tactless in their criticisms. If they are not careful, 8s can be consumed by greed, and their leadership can become controlling if they don't put their trust in others and delegate.

When the number 8 appears, it's a sign from the universe that abundance is coming your way, and you will achieve it if you put in the effort. 8 reminds you that your angel will always guide, support, and encourage you, so you don't need to fret even when you encounter challenges. Trust in yourself and the universe, and you'll receive the abundance in store.

Nine

Number 9 is linked to old souls, those who have gone through life and learned all they think they could learn from it. 9s are compassionate, understanding, and accepting, and are known for their humanitarian and altruistic pursuits. 9s can be generous to a fault, and they enjoy sharing what they know with others. However, they can struggle with learning from new situations, and they can get lost in fantasy. Mitigating this disconnection is paramount, as it can lead to an escape from reality if unchecked.

If number 9 appears to you, it is the universe's reminder to take time and reflect on your life and the path you need to take. You will have your angel's support in future hardships, so you need to follow your intuition.

Takeaway

In this chapter, we've explored:

- The Pythagorean alphanumeric cipher

- The calculation of Destiny and Life Path Numbers

- The meaning of single digit numbers and interpretations of single digit angel numbers

Chapter 6

Number Sequences and Combinations

"The magnitude of life is overwhelming. Angels are here to help us take it peace by peace."
~ Terri Guillemets

In this chapter, we'll dive into the meanings of the most visible angel numbers, whose presence casts no doubt that the universe is communicating with you. Master numbers, repeating sequences, and consecutive numbers make up just a tiny part of the vast universe of angel numbers, and they are great peeks into the universe's intentions. However, as you become more in tune with Source, the numbers will shift and morph into mixed sequences, some that may not register if you're not in tune with the universe. We'll explore these numbers in the next chapter, so for now, let's get to it!

Master Numbers

The vibration contained within angel numbers is significant, and the appearance of these numbers always brings some force into our lives. However, some numbers hold significantly more power and take the power of their root numbers to new heights. In numerology, these are identified as Master Numbers, and they include the numbers 11, 22, and 33. If you get these three numbers while calculating your Destiny and Life Path Numbers, don't reduce them to their single digits. Your power lies in the Master Numbers, and your soul needs to match and transcend its purpose and destiny.

Because the numbers 1, 2, and 3 constitute the Triangle of Enlightenment, Master Numbers are said to symbolize the three stages of creation, with 11 representing Envision, 22 representing Building or Creating, and 33 representing Sharing.

Master Number 11: The Master Visionary

Master Number 11 draws on the power of number 2 (1+1=2), but it is also heavily influenced by the vibration of number 1, creating a powerful vibration that embodies spiritual awareness and enlightenment, sensitivity, and leadership. The appearance of 11 is the universe's sign that you need to pay closer attention to your thoughts and ideas, as they may contain the answers to attaining your desires. The universe is calling for you to trust your intuition and gut instinct, and you need to take a moment to introspect and rely on your spiritual inner voice.

Master Number 22: The Master Builder

Drawing on the power of Master Number 11 and its single-digit virtue, 4, Master Number 22's vibration is a formidable force that can turn even the grandest dreams into reality. Master Number 22 combines the ideas and visions of 11 with the structure, practicality, and logic of 4, transforming these ideas into realities through well-crafted plans of action and a systematic approach to solving problems and overcoming hurdles. However, there's a risk of going too far and getting lost in the pursuit of the material, which may destroy the creations. Conversely, 22s may ignore the power of their Master Number and get consumed by idleness and lack of direction.

The appearance of 22 is the universe's sign that you need to look at the bigger picture, then work on the details to realize this vision. It is a reminder to remain positive and optimistic as you work to realize your manifestations, both in the material and spiritual planes.

Master Number 33: The Master Teacher

The vibration of Master Number 33 is otherworldly potent, and its power makes it difficult for 33s to live up to their abilities and master themselves. Master Number 33 draws on the powers of Master Number 11, Master Number 22, and its single virtue, number 6. 33s are the universe's channel for divine messages, as they are the guides who lead others to their healing and enlightenment. Master Number 33 has the visionary and builder of 11 and 22, but the humility and compassion of 6 make them great helpers to those looking to bring their ideas to fruition. However, they can be prone to overthinking, and they can be highly critical and judgmental.

The power of the vibration of Master Number 33 is so great that its presence in your life is the universe's signal that whatever positive changes or projects you may be considering will be worth your while. The universe is also making a promise that you will always receive assistance in your undertaking.

Repeating Sequences

Repeating sequences are what many people recognize as angel numbers because they are so easy to spot. And because of this, your angel will communicate through repeating sequences when your vibration starts aligning with the universe. Let's explore double- to quadruple-digit repeating sequences:

Repeating 0's - 00; 000; 0000

0 is the number that captures the vibration of everything, and nothing. It is Source, and the appearance of 0s is a gentle reminder to trust the universe. It is a sign that everything has come full circle, and you are one with Source. 0 assures you of your angel's presence and calls for you to be more vigilant of signs from the universe, and to heed the universe's message when it appears.

Repeating 1's - 111; 1111

1 embodies the vibration of creation, of new starts and new paths. The appearance of 1's is the universe's sign that you need to stop and focus on your thoughts and ideas. Are your thoughts positive or negative? If you are thinking negatively, work on shifting the thoughts to a more positive vibration, and you will manifest what you are thinking of, negative or positive.

For most people, 111 or 1111 is the number they see most. This is the universe showing you that you are in alignment with Source. It is a "thumbs up" from the universe and an encouragement to keep your vibration high. Once you start seeing 1's, it won't be long before you begin noticing other angel numbers as well.

Repeating 2's - 222; 2222

2 is the number of harmony, and seeing 2's is the universe's way of letting you know that you need to keep going, but you must be patient because your manifestation is on its way. The universe is encouraging you, providing assurance that your efforts are not for nothing, and that positive thoughts, a positive attitude, and positive affirmations of your efforts will pay off. Don't rush things; instead, focus on the slow and sure path to your goal.

Repeating 3's - 333; 3333

33 denotes the Master Teacher, and 3 is known to refer to Ascended Masters, the great teachers who existed. When 3's appear, the universe is reminding you of the close presence of your guardians, who love and support you. 3 is also the number of the trinity - mind, body, and soul. If you're struggling with alignment, the presence of 3 is a call for you to dive deeper into your spiritual self to find the balance that you need to realize your manifestation. Through it all, your guardians are close and ready to offer guidance and support.

Repeating 4's - 44; 444; 4444

4 is the number of stability, and when the universe communicates through repeating 4's, it's a sign that you are safe.

Your guardians are all around you, keeping you cocooned in their love and support. As you work on making your dreams a reality, your angels are keeping watch over you, ensuring that you are safe. Repeating 4's also serve as an encouragement, a call for you to trust yourself to do your part.

Repeating 5's - 55; 555; 5555

When you start seeing 5's, the universe is bringing to your awareness that a big shift is coming in your life. You are destined to see major changes, which may appear unexpectedly fast. This is your chance, not to cower in fear, but to shed your limitations and find it in yourself to thrive through the changes. To find your strength and passion to put in the work, and not give up.

Repeating 6's - 66; 666; 6666

Repeating 6's is a sign from the universe that your balance is off, and you are focused too much on the material. For many of us, 666 is supposed to be the number we all avoid, as it's supposed to signify a bad omen. This cannot be further from the truth. 666, and the repeating 6's, are the universe's way of letting you know that you need to reach for balance. You are neglecting a part of you, usually the spiritual side, and you need to work on reclaiming that balance even as you reach for your goals. Focus on the positive, and remember that you have the support and love of your guardians, and all you need to do is ask for their help.

Repeating 7's - 77; 777; 7777

When 7's start appearing to you, it is a message from the universe that your efforts are about to pay off. The universe has acknowledged the path you are on, assuring you that you are on the right path. Maintain the positive attitude, and rest assured that more good things are coming your way. Double down on your current path, and keep your alignment with your guardians and the universe. You're bound to receive your rewards.

Repeating 8's - 88; 888; 8888

When the universe sends repeating 8's, it is an assurance that abundance is on its way. It is the universe's way of letting you know that your past efforts and hard work did not go unnoticed, and you're about to reap the fruits of your labor. But this is not a call to relax and take it easy. It is a call to keep up the good work, stay the course, and believe that you have the strength in you to overcome any challenges that may present themselves. Your guardians are watching over you, and you can always rejoice in knowing that you have their support.

Repeating 9's - 99; 999; 9999

Repeating 9's is a sign from the universe that you need to live your Life's Purpose. You need to align with your true self and share your gifts and abilities with the world. Lead by example as you blaze the trail toward your destiny. The appearance of 9's lets you know the time has come for you to reach your full potential. You need to believe in yourself, trust the universe, and rise above your limitations to reach your goal.

Ascending Sequences

As we've mentioned before, the arrangement of the digits in a sequence is also important, as it helps to accurately interpret the messages sent by the universe. Each digit lends its vibration to the sequence, and looking into each digit's vibration is undoubtedly helpful. However, the placement of each digit influences the overall message of the sequence. Let's explore a few ascending sequences that you may come across:

123

This number signifies progression, a sign from the universe that your life is changing, whether you're ready for it or not. The arrangement of the numbers shows that this change will be worth it, as it will involve a systematic progression from one manifestation to the next. 123 is a beautiful message from the universe, and you need to be ready to embrace the changes and believe in your ability to overcome the challenges that may appear in your path.

1234

1234 is the universe's message that you will realize your dreams. You have the support of the angels on your path, and by putting in the work needed, you will realize what you are seeking to achieve, step by step. Things might get difficult, but you need to remain relentless, work hard, and your progress will be clear.

1212

This number is the universe's encouraging message urging you to strive for your highest ideals. What have you been putting off because you're scared or not ready? What are you waiting for? This number is a sign from the universe that your undertakings will have positive outcomes. So, you must find your strength, focus on the positive, and take the leap. Your angel will always be there to guide and support you.

1919

The embodiment of creativity and hard work, 1919 is a sign from the universe that while you will finally find your way to your manifestation, you need to be ready for the path ahead. The journey will not be smooth, and you may feel like you are drowning, but the appearance of 1919 is the universe's sign that you are on the right path, and have the creativity and resilience to forge through. Believe in yourself.

3377

3377 promises peace in your life, peace that is gained from your unwavering trust in the universe. It is a sign that calls for you to be ready to embrace the good that manifests in your life. Let go of the things in your life holding you back and keeping you from achieving your potential. Prioritize your inner peace, and don't chase material possessions to the point of neglecting your journey to spiritual enlightenment.

456

Drawing on the stability of 4, the freedom of 5, and the domesticity of 6, 456 is the universe's sign that your expansion is imminent, but you need to keep a watchful eye on the relationships in your life, as they will be transforming. As you keep growing, do not overlook the relationships in your life, and take the time to take care of any issues that may come up. Offer your loved ones the attention they desire, as you may have overlooked their needs as you pursue your dreams.

456 is also the universe's way of telling us to be aware of other signs guiding our path.

4747

4747 is the universe's sign urging you to ease the grip you have on your life. You need to let go of your need to control everything in your life. 4747 calls for you to find the balance between control and letting go. If you are struggling to maintain control over everything, this shows your reluctance to place your trust in the universe. Choose to do what you need, but give the universe a chance to help you by relinquishing control.

5789

Our thoughts and beliefs reflect our own experiences, and sometimes it gets difficult to step back and understand that others may be right too. 5789 is the universe's sign that we need to take a moment and consider the perceptions of others. We may be too rigid in our thoughts, which will hinder our ability and chance to explore options that may serve our grand purpose. 5789 is the universe's call to us to be more open-minded.

678

678 is the universe's sign that your spiritual journey will bring you abundance both in the spiritual and material. Through the appearance of this number, you are receiving encouragement to focus on your spiritual growth. This focus and engagement with

your spiritual side will pay off, so don't give up hope or faith even as challenges appear in your way.

6789

6789 is the number of self-love and self-acceptance. The universe is calling for you to revel in who you are, and to embrace who you are. It is a sign for you to realize that you are complete and that any changes you seek should not be from a position of lack, but from a genuine desire to grow. 6789 calls for you to connect with the Divine and devote your time to your spiritual journey and passions.

Descending Sequences

Descending sequences, for the most part, call for us to switch our focus from the external to our internal selves. Many signs call for introspection, for us to grow our thoughts, feelings, and spirituality to connect with the Divine. Descending sequences still hold powerful vibrations, so don't let the title fool you into thinking they may be "less than" ascending sequences.

Let's explore some sequences that you may come across in your manifestation journey:

1010

Angel Number 1010 is the universe's sign that you're about to experience significant change, and that your manifestation is approaching at a significant pace. However, you need to be careful about your thoughts and feelings, as negativity will manifest in your reality just as quickly. 1010 calls for you to introspect and tap into your intuitive abilities.

2211

2211 is the universe's call for you to turn your focus to what you desire and be clear about what you want to manifest. By affirming this clarity, the universe confirms your desire, even if your manifestation is already unfolding. 2211 also encourages you to be more open-minded and willing to see things from a different perspective. The universe is calling for you to trust yourself and look inward for answers.

2121

With the angel number 2121, the universe is notifying you that you are about to experience a calm period of your life. This is a call for you to embrace and appreciate the equilibrium that is part of your life and express gratitude for the blessings you have received from the universe so far.

321

321 is the universe's reminder that you have divine guidance, and that you need to embrace this guidance even if things are going your way. 321 is also the universe's call for you to let go of the past and things that don't serve your manifestation. Release the negativity and the things holding you back. This will allow you to make space for the opportunities and blessings that the universe sends your way.

432

432 is the universe's assurance that divine help is here for you as you face and overcome challenges. Even when you make mistakes, you can lean on divine guidance to help you make amends and maneuver the new situation. However, 432 calls for you to release the negative energy that has a chokehold on you, as it is stopping you from realizing your manifestation. Pay attention to your recurrent thoughts, feelings, dreams, and visions, and turn your focus to your creative endeavors.

4321

4321 is the universe's call for you to release the negativity hindering your manifestation. The universe is asking you to let go of the things stopping you from pursuing your dreams. You need to find your way home, home to the creation embodied in the number 1. Your guardians have your back, and while it may be scary to let go of the comfortable and reach for the unknown, you cannot achieve progress without shedding a few layers you've accumulated throughout your life. Take the plunge and make your way back to creation.

5322

This number is a sign of healing and spiritual growth. It is the universe's message that you can find your way through your hurt and pain and find healing, happiness, and peace. This healing process can be slow and painful, and the universe will always show you that your guardians are with you, offering support and help. Healing and spiritual growth take time, so you need to embrace patience as you take baby steps in your journey. Don't give up when it gets difficult; instead, lean on your angel. Allow your guardians to help you as you open up your world to bolder, happier, and more relaxed experiences.

654

With this number, the universe is calling for you to follow your intuition and the guidance of the intuitive messages you have been receiving about the changes in your life. These changes are meant to guide you to manifest your blessings, rewards, and prayers. The appearance of 654 is the universe's assurance that your efforts toward achieving your manifestations have not gone to waste. Your efforts have manifested new opportunities and circumstances, and it's time to trust the universe as it lays out the changes you need to make. Express gratitude to Divine Source when this number appears, and stay positive throughout the manifestation of the changes.

875

875 is the universe's sign that you need to slow down, take a breather, and find your balance. It is the universe's reminder that your manifestation is unfolding and a warning that any drastic changes may influence the outcome of your manifestation. Take this time to nurture your body and spirit and to find that much-needed mind, body, and soul balance that fosters alignment with Divine Source. This number asks that you embrace moderation and slow your pursuit of the material.

8750

The number 8750 is a message from the Divine that you need to turn your focus from the external and instead turn inwards for answers. 8750 calls for us to create a habit of reflecting on the decisions and choices we make, not to point out any mistakes or highlight our greatness, but to connect with our life choices and decisions. This number also lets you know that it's okay to have doubts, but don't wallow in them. Your doubts are a sign that you need to call on Divine Source for guidance.

We can never explore all the sequences and combinations present in the universe, as they are vast as the infinite existence of Divine Source. Instead, I will give you the tools to interpret the sequences that may appear to you that we haven't covered in this book. In the next chapter, we'll explore how to interpret sequences, and we'll take a look at a few more numbers that appear more frequently.

Takeaway

In this chapter, we've explored:

- The vibration of Master Numbers

- The vibration repeating sequences, from repeating 1's to repeating 9's

- The vibration of Ascending Sequences, including examples of frequently occurring Ascending Sequences

- The vibration of Descending Sequences, including examples of frequently occurring Descending Sequences

Chapter 7

Interpreting Numbers

"Alas, none of our divine revelations arrive with footnotes or explanations."

~ Imam Jamal Rahman

We've highlighted how to interpret angel numbers a few times in the book, but let me cover it once more so we can explore more numbers and see how you can find ways of interpreting angel numbers that don't appear often. As you learn to trust Divine Source more implicitly and follow your intuitive guidance, interpreting the numbers will become easier. This is not because you'll have gotten used to seeing angel numbers, but because your spirit guide will almost always whisper the message in your soul. When I see angel numbers these days, it never takes long to figure out what Divine Source is communicating. When angel numbers appear, and you have embraced intentional living and intuitive guidance, you are always aware of what the universe is trying to communicate. You are already aware of what you are struggling with and what questions you've asked, and angel numbers assure you that the universe's support is available. So, when you take a moment to think about the number, you can feel your soul's tranquility as you decode the message.

I love seeing angel numbers, as I always seem to find a new lesson when I introspect. I find areas of my life I have neglected, lessons I forgot, or blessings I somehow overlooked. Let's explore how to interpret the numbers that appear to you:

Single Digit Virtues

The interpretation of single-digit virtues is straightforward, which makes understanding these interpretations essential in interpreting any other numbers that appear. We've already explored the vibrations of single-digit virtues, so please remember to refer to them often, even if you think you don't need to.

Repeating Numbers

When a number recurs in the angel number sequence, its

vibration is the essence of the message. This repetition doesn't need to be sequential, though. Interpreting repeating numbers is also relatively easy, as you only need to focus on the vibrations of the single virtues contained within the sequence.

For example, interpreting 15:15 only requires you to understand the vibration of 1 and 5. From here, you know that the universe is assuring you that your new path, or creation, will bring about adventure and freedom in your life. It is an assurance that your new path will be worth it, as it will show you a new side of yourself and free you from what has been holding you back.

In the same way, seeing 11:55 still communicates that your new path will be to freedom, but the message is more amplified, and your manifestation will be more impactful. This is because the combined vibration of the digits amplifies the power of the manifestation. 11:55 means that you should expect major changes, requiring you to embrace the universe's support as these changes manifest.

It's these seemingly tiny shifts that make Angel Numbers so magical, and interpretation unique to each of us. Using 11:55 again, imagine you are working through a challenging project at work or you're working through turbulent emotions. The appearance of 11:55 is a message of assurance from the universe, a reminder that you are creating something new, and it will all be worth it. It is a call to remain steadfast and not give up. If your life has been stagnant for a while and you see 11:55, this is the universe's call to prepare yourself for a new path. Change is coming, and with it, the surprises of number 5, which means you need to brace yourself for what's coming your way. This is why our situations and circumstances matter when interpreting angel numbers. You can use interpretations provided on the internet, but you'll soon start relying more on your intuitive interpretation.

Mixed Numbers

Mixed numbers are marginally harder to spot, and we only become aware of them when they repeatedly show up. Sometime back, the number 1936 kept popping up. I use the 24-hour clock format, and for about two weeks, I seemed drawn to the clock at 19:36. The first two times, it didn't really register. When it happened the third time, I was sure I was remembering the digits wrong. So I asked the universe for clarity, and two days later, my grocery shopping totaled $19.36 after I'd used a few coupons. There's no way I'd have doctored that, and I settled in the bliss of recognizing the universe's message.

I had seen such mixed numbers before, but it had been quite a while. At the time, the appearance of 3 and 6 was somewhat expected, as I'd been reflecting more on my relationships and emotional responses. With 1 and 9, however, I knew that I was finally on the cusp of a major breakthrough. At the time, I was struggling with compassion towards some family members. One of my aunts was going through a hard time, but I was finding it difficult to sympathize or show kindness because of all the "bad things" she'd done. When I was told about her difficult time, my first thought was, "serves her right." I was attributing it all to karma, payback for all the pain and misery she'd inflicted on almost every member of the family.

However, as I was recounting all the "evil" deeds she'd committed to justify my lack of empathy to one of my friends, I was engulfed by an enormous wave of guilt. I was drowning in the murky depths of the feeling, and I burst into tears. I had to end the call and curl up on the couch. I cried myself to sleep, and when I woke up, the clock read 00:36. And I just knew. With double zeros, the vibration of 3 and 6 was magnified, and I just went to my desk and journaled. I wrote everything I felt about my aunt, all the perceived wrongs, and finished with the question, "Isn't this all the more reason to be compassionate?"

About a month later, I started seeing 19:36, and I understood that my reflection, introspection, and work were paying off. I'd done what I could to help my aunt, despite the lingering bitterness still stuck in my soul.

In many cases, seeing mixed numbers will not really happen out of the blue. Instead, these sequences will build upon previous sequences, making it easier to spot them. For example, you will have been exposed to multiple 6's before the universe sends the sequence 1236 your way. In other situations, even though the sequence may seem unconnected, the individual numbers will have some relationship that makes them unique enough to register in your mind. For example, with 1936, 6 and 9 are multiples of 3. And with my angel number predominantly featuring repeating 1's, I was bound to notice.

Once you've spotted the mixed sequence, interpreting it can be done in various ways:

Reducing the sequence to its single virtue

This is similar to the process of determining our Life Path and Destiny Numbers. If your Angel Number is an unfamiliar mixed sequence, reducing the sequence to its single virtue will help you to understand its encompassing vibration. For example;

1936 reduces to $1 + 9 + 3 + 6 = 19$

18 reduces to $1 + 9 = 10; 1 + 0 = 1$

The Angel Number 1936's encompassing vibration is that of

number 1, which denotes new beginnings, creation, and new direction on your journey. Interpreting your angel numbers this way will give you a glimpse into the messages the universe is sending, and while it is okay if you stop there, you might fail to get the entirety of the message.

Focusing on the vibration of the individual digits in the sequence

I love this method because this is how I trained myself to understand the vibrations of each digit without needing to refer to my notes over and over again. This method also helped me understand my relationships with the vibrations of each number, and my interpretations have become more in tune with my situations. This took time, and it was made possible by the alignment work I did, finding ways to be in alignment with the universe.

In this method, you focus on each digit's vibration and decode the overall message from that. Let's use 1936 again;

1 - New beginnings, creation, forging a new path.

9 - Empathy, altruism, compassion, experience.

3 - Communication, self-expression, creativity.

6 - Domesticity, caring for others, nurturing.

For every single one of us, the interpretations we draw from these vibrations will be different. Once you have the vibrations, take time to introspect and find the connection between the vibrations and your experiences. For me, the message was that of expressing compassion to someone I believe did not deserve it.

It's important to take the time to meditate and introspect when your angel number appears, because even if you get the same number, your experiences will not always be the same every time. The nuances in the messages shift to match who you are in that moment. Journal your angel number interpretations, and you'll grow to understand the vibrations with greater ease each time.

Focusing on the connection of the vibrations of the sequence

The more I used the previous method, the more I felt like something was missing from my interpretations. Yes, I was making progress, but it seemed like I was working with incomplete information. I often found myself stumped and stalling, unsure of my steps. When I started mindful journaling, I began noticing how my experiences kept shifting with my alignment. I was more in tune with my emotions, and even when I saw repeating sequences, I could feel a difference in the messages I understood. Repeating sequences became less about the individual numbers and more about the vibrational shift I experienced when I saw them.

That's when it occurred to me - my interpretations felt incomplete because I was not considering how the vibrations in each sequence relate to each other. Think of how your mannerisms, speech, and behavior shift subtly depending on who you are with. The same happens with the vibrations of each digit. They come together to form a base vibration, but there are still shifts and changes to each vibration, creating new interpretations of the message each time. Now, my interpretations factor in the base vibration, the individual vibration, and how these vibrations are connected to each other and to my vibration.

Let's use 1936 again. The vibrations of 9 and 6 embody emotions of nurture and compassion, with 3 encompassing self-expression and communication. 1 is the number of creation. Because 1 is the first vibration, the universe is promising that something new is coming. From here, your experience colors the rest of the vibration. This angel number, for me, was a message of encouragement because of the internal work I was already doing, a call for me to show compassion and care to the person I wasn't willing to. I had to choose to communicate my compassion, something I had never done before. Ultimately, I created a new relationship with my aunt, one filled with compassion and healthy boundaries that allowed me to protect my family.

Interpreting angel numbers is a fun, exciting experience, and it should be undertaken as an adventure, not an obligation. Because of your vibrational alignment with Divine Source, frustration will be counterintuitive, as it lowers your vibration. So, embark on your interpretation journey with an open mind, heart, and soul. Allow the momentum of your vibration to guide your interpretation, and enjoy the journey, as the manifestation is already unfolding.

Takeaway

In this chapter, we've explored:

- The interpretation of single virtue vibrations

- The interpretation of repeating sequences

- The three ways of interpreting the vibration of mixed sequences

Chapter 8

Angel Numbers and Manifesting

"It's unlimited what the universe can bring when you understand the great secret that thoughts become things."
~ Fearless Soul; Nicholas Macri (songwriter)

If you have any experience with the Law of Attraction, the concept of manifestation is not new to you. Essentially, manifestation is the premise that **"your thoughts create your reality."** Manifestation is your thoughts culminating in your experiences in the physical world. I'll quickly recap the manifestation process before diving into how you can use angel numbers to manifest your desired reality.

Manifesting Your Desired Reality - How To

The process of manifesting your desires can seem simple at first glance, but anyone who has immersed themselves in this practice knows there is a lot that goes into it. If you've ever heard the words, "still waters run deep," please believe that this wholly applies to the manifestation process. Let's explore what manifesting entails:

Clearly express your desire

The first step in manifesting is to ask. What is it you desire? However, you cannot just offer a vague request. You need to clearly define your desire, and the more details you can add, the better. Asking for "abundance," while commendable, is too broad and vague. However, asking for a job that allows you to live comfortably, both financially and socially, is much better. If you are unsure what you desire most, take time to reflect on your life. With a pen and paper, write out how you want to live, what you need to get there, and how you can get there. From here, it will be easier to pinpoint your true desires.

With this first step, be careful not to be swayed by external forces. Do not be pressured by societal ideas, feelings of jealousy and envy, or even your belief that you need to have achieved something "by now." Rather, lean into who you are, your own soul and instinct. During your introspection, you will uncover your true desires, and these should be what drive what you ask for.

Set your intentions

As we've mentioned quite a few times in this book, vibrational alignment is essential in manifesting your desires. In this stage of the manifestation process, you need to be mindful of your thoughts, words, and beliefs. Setting your intentions involves using powerful statements to raise and focus your vibration on your desires. Your vibration should match the desire, not oppose it.

Let's imagine your desire is to be promoted at work. In this stage, your thoughts should reflect your belief in your abilities to handle that role well. However, if your thoughts are filled with examples of why you wouldn't get the promotion, or how you lack the skills compared to another coworker, your vibration will be that of lack. Your desire and beliefs are in opposition, which pretty much kills your chances of manifesting your desired reality. Instead, your reality will reflect your thoughts; that is, you will live a reality that affirms your lack of skills and inability to handle the new role.

Setting your intentions is the hardest part of manifestation, as it requires your unwavering focus on the contents of your mind. Keep your thoughts positive, and if you find this difficult, employ the help of affirmations, visualization, journaling, a gratitude practice, and meditation. The aim is to achieve alignment with the universe and your desired reality.

Take Inspired Action

Your intentions and vibration in check, it is now time to do your part. Inspired action is taking the steps necessary to make your dream a reality. And this is where angel numbers have the most impact. Angel numbers are powerful tools of guidance and clarity, making them great companions when it comes to taking the path that will get you to your desires. The messages relayed through angel numbers usually confirm that we're on the right path, warn that we may encounter difficulties, provide support through the hard times, encouragement to keep going, and guidance through new paths and directions.

Inspired action and intentions work simultaneously, as your vibrational alignment allows you to lean into the power of the universe as you do your best to make your dream a reality. Alignment makes angel numbers visible, and your actions need to embody the universe's guidance for your desires to manifest.

Trust and Let Go

The first time I saw that letting go was part of the manifestation process, I was confused. After all, didn't I just set my intentions in the second stage? However, the more you practice, the more you realize how important letting go is to the manifestation process. In the manifestation process, letting go is a sign that you trust the universe to bring your desire forth. When you focus on the manifestation, constantly wondering when it will happen, you skew your vibration. This, in turn, makes it harder for the universe to grant your wish because your anxious anticipation is bound to breed doubt in your mind. This is a destructive self-feeding cycle that will keep your manifestation at bay, which in turn creates greater frustration in you, further skewing your vibration.

Letting go means trusting that the universe will grant your desires at its pleasure - which is usually the right time. Letting go means your focus on the journey, enjoying the work you do, the efforts you put in, and expressing gratitude for all that the universe has granted you thus far. Letting go of the manifestation means that you are confident in the universe's power and willingness to grant your desire.

Manifesting with Angel Numbers - The Basics

In the same way journaling, meditation, visualization, and practicing gratitude give more power to your vibration and aid in manifestation, angel numbers are a powerful tool in your manifestation arsenal. Angel numbers add immense power to steps two and three of manifesting, as they help focus your intention and guide your actions. Angel numbers appear whenever we are in alignment, but you can call on the universe to help you out when you have a burning desire you want to manifest and need all the help you can get.

- **Ask your guardian angel for help**

If you need something, the first step is to ask. The universe is always willing and ready to answer our questions and grant us our requests, and you shouldn't hesitate to reach out. The appearance of angel numbers puts us at ease, allays our fears, and assures us that Divine Source has our back. If you need the universe's assurance as you work towards your manifestation, don't feel like this need is casting a shadow over your vibration. Lean into that feeling and ask the universe for guidance. You can ask for the appearance of a certain number, or you can ask the universe to show you the way.

- **Keep an eye out for repeating number sequences**

Once you have asked, you need to stay vigilant. Keep working on keeping your vibration aligned with the universe, and don't lose hope if you don't see the sequences immediately. Keep working, and pay attention to any repeating number sequences you encounter.

Trust that the universe will respond to your request, and don't get frustrated if the appearance of angel numbers takes time. If you feel like you have stopped seeing angel numbers, refer to chapter four to reacquaint yourself with reasons why angel numbers may not be appearing, and how to increase your awareness.

- **Use the interpretations of received angel numbers to focus your intentions**

The appearance of angel numbers is the universe's assurance that your request was received, and that it's the right time to send you guidance. Once you've received the universe's communication, take time to interpret the message, and use the interpretation to fuel your focus. Whether it's a message of guidance, support, or warning, revel in the fact that Divine Source is with you, and that your angel has your back no matter what you may be experiencing at that time.

- **Keep trusting that angels are in your corner**

As your manifestation unfolds, don't lose faith in Divine Source and your guardian angel(s). The universe is always supporting you, even if it doesn't seem so in the moment. Keep leaning on Divine help, and when doubts threaten to creep in, remind yourself that your angel will never abandon you or steer you wrong. Faith and trust in Divine Source is the air that feeds the embers of your manifestation, even as frustration and doubt threaten your alignment.

Manifesting with Angel Numbers - Rituals

Because of the interpretations connected to certain angel numbers, they are connected to various manifestations. For example, number 8 is mainly linked to abundance - usually financial abundance. 6 is mainly associated with domesticity, and by extension, romantic love. 1 is the number of changes and new beginnings, while 7 is the manifestation of spiritual growth. In your manifestation journey, you can also include certain rituals to encourage the appearance of angel numbers whose interpretations match your desire.

- **Paper Tracing and Pillow Method**

This involves taking a pen and paper and, without lifting the pen, writing the desired angel number over and over again until the page is filled. The first time, the number should span the entirety of the paper, and then just keep tracing until you have filled the page. Some numbers will be easier to trace than others, so be patient and don't rush the process. This focus helps to raise and focus your vibration, drawing your manifestation closer.

Once the paper is filled, fold it neatly and place it under your pillow. Sleep with the paper under your pillow for a week, and your manifestation will unfold.

- **Charge your Wrist**

If you're like me, you look at your wrists countless times a day. So when something's written on it, you'll be drawn to it for most of your waking day. This means that what's written will be dominant in your mind, focusing your intentions. By writing an angel number on your wrist, you can send the energy out into the universe or open yourself up to receiving the energy. If your intention is to send out a vibration of love into the universe, write the Angel Number associated with love - 6, 222, 212, 33, etc. - on your dominant wrist. If your desire is to receive love, write the number sequence on your non-dominant wrist. Whichever desire you have, charging your wrist is a great way to boost your vibrational alignment and focus your intention.

- **Charge your Water (or Beverages)**

Your water bottle or beverage containers can also be great tools to help you set your intentions. Write your desired angel number on the container or bottle, and bless the drink before consuming it. This way, you charge the beverage with your desired intention, boosting your vibration every time you drink from the container or bottle.

- **Post the Numbers in Relevant Places**

You've probably come across texts that encourage you to post affirmations on mirrors or places you tend to look at multiple times a day. This works in the same way. Posting the numbers in relevant places - like placing a post-it note on your computer with numbers 4, 404, or 22 for structure and discipline in your work or number 8 or 808 in your wallet for financial abundance - will charge your intentions, helping you focus your vibration on your desires.

- **Angel Numbers as Mantra**

Repetition is a great way to keep your mind focused on something and absorb it. Repeating angel numbers as mantras (chanting in your head or out loud) focuses your vibration on that desire, and charges your vibration to align with your desired manifestation. To make it even more powerful, start the mantra when you are in a meditative state, as your mind will be more receptive to the message and less likely to throw doubts at you.

Always remember that you cannot force the universe to provide answers before the time is right. These actions are meant to charge your vibration, to put you in a state where your vibration is such that the universe responds with ease. When you are in receptive mode, the universe is encouraged to reward you, and your manifestations will be faster, more potent, and free-flowing.

Takeaway

In this chapter, we've explored:

- The steps to manifesting your desires
- How to incorporate Angel Numbers into your manifestation journey
- Angel Number rituals to help charge your vibration for faster manifestation

Chapter 9

Manifesting with Specific Numbers

"When you reach for the thought that feels better, the universe is now responding differently to you because of that effort. And so, the things that follow you get better and better, too."
~ Abraham Hicks

Using scripting techniques for manifesting is a phenomenal way to raise your vibration and focus your intention when you find yourself in a tight spot. Scripting techniques vary in intensity and time, but there are a few things you need to remember before you start:

- **Your state of mind:** If you're frustrated, anxious, or desperate for an answer, scripting will not be of much help. Scripting techniques piggyback on your vibrational energy, and if you are not calm and relaxed, all you'll build on is the erratic vibration that you've already amassed. So, before you sit and start writing, ensure that you are calm and relaxed, and have no doubts swirling in your mind.

- **Location:** A quiet room where you will remain undisturbed for about half an hour to an hour is recommended, as scripting requires uninterrupted focus. You also need a comfortable seat and desk with adequate lighting. The room shouldn't be too bright, though, as you may go into a meditative trance during scripting, and harsh lighting makes it almost impossible.

- **Time:** You need to choose a time when you have no obligations clamoring for your attention. Scripting time should be uninterrupted, so you need to be able to turn off electronics and focus on the page in front of you for half an hour or more. Also, choose a time when you are relaxed and calm, but still alert, when your vibration can easily be raised by the affirmation on your page.

- **Tools:** A blank page and pen are all you need for scripting, although I'd recommend having a manifestation journal for this purpose because this practice will always be something you indulge in time and time again.

Scripting for manifestation is focused on one desire at a time, and you cannot change the affirmation you choose, as this will break the vibrational energy of your set intention. What is it you want to manifest? Once you have your request, create a short, concise, and positive affirmation that expresses your desire ***as if*** it has already come true.

Let's explore a few scripting techniques to showcase what I mean.

222 Scripting Technique

Also known as the 22x2 Manifestation Method, the 222 scripting technique is a two-day manifestation practice that will boost your vibration when you need your manifestation to unfold a little faster. With this method, your intention will be laser-focused because of the repetition involved, which for some, can feel a bit too much. The practice is pretty simple - all you need to do is write out your affirmation/desired manifestation 22 times for two consecutive days.

Remember, the affirmation should be positive, short, concise, and ***as if.*** For example, if your desire is to be more assertive, your affirmation can read, "I stand up for myself, my beliefs, and boundaries without remorse." Or, if you are breaking away from limiting thoughts and behaviors, you can write, "I am free of the thoughts and behaviors that hold me back."

Once you have your affirmation, write it in your journal 22 times. As you write, do not mindlessly go through the motions just to finish. Instead, focus on the emotion your manifestation will evoke in you. Feel the triumph of standing up for yourself, and the joy of your mind accepting that you are capable of so much more. See yourself in that situation, conquering your doubts and fears and coming out of it triumphantly. As you write each line, revel in the feeling of your manifestation coming to life. As you get drawn deeper into the emotion, you may enter a meditative trance and stop writing. Don't force yourself to get back to it. Enjoy the feeling until you slowly return to the present moment, and keep writing until you are done.

On the second day, do the same. Write out your affirmation and indulge in the feeling of your manifested reality. This is the perfect technique for those times when you don't have so much time to dedicate to scripting but need a vibrational boost.

444 Scripting Technique

The 444 scripting technique, also known as the 44x4 Manifestation Method, is a more intensive scripting technique that spans four days. The basic premise discussed in the 222 scripting technique holds true here, and the only difference is the number of lines and days. Each day, for four days, write out your affirmation 44 times.

555 Scripting Technique

Following the two previous techniques, you can tell what's coming next. As you've probably guessed, this is a five-day scripting technique that involves writing your affirmation 55 times each day. The increased frequency and time are important because the intensity of your vibration will be influenced by the time you dedicate to the practice.

Think about it this way - in two days, you can only increase the momentum of a vibration that was already high, otherwise, you won't get anything out of the practice. Two days is sufficient for a manifestation that was already unfolding, and all you needed was a slight push to raise your vibration even higher to boost your alignment. A five-day practice, on the other hand, can help focus and raise your low vibration. Five days is enough to help you conquer those lingering doubts, raise your vibration, and seal your trust in the universe. Your affirmations are intense as well, and the time taken to write them out is longer, allowing you to sink deeper into the feeling of manifestation. This technique requires dedication, trust in the universe, and unwavering trust in your own ability to stick to the practice.

777 Scripting Method

This is my favorite scripting method, mainly because it incorporates the angel number associated with hope, spiritual enlightenment, and introspection. Writing an affirmation 77 times for seven days is no easy feat, and it took me months before I was able to undertake the practice to the end without failing at least once. The 777 scripting method has come in handy when my vibration has been wonky, and I've always used it whenever I need divine help with my spiritual journey.

If you're new to scripting, I wouldn't advise starting with this because of the amount of dedication it requires. Start small, with the 222 or 333 scripting method, and build from there.

369 Scripting Technique

This scripting technique is another one I love practicing because of the dedication it requires and the long-term changes it has on my vibrational alignment. Despite its length of time, this scripting method is still meant to bring one manifestation into being. The 369 scripting method is perfect for bigger manifestations, the desires bound to effect a massive change in your life, internally and externally. I use the 369 method when I am trying to adopt a new habit or lifestyle change.

The 369 method is a three-times-a-day practice that involves writing your affirmation three times in the morning, preferably upon waking up; six times during the day; and nine times at night, just before you go to bed. The power of this method lies in how your vibration is charged throughout the day. When you wake up and write your affirmations, your day starts with the vibrational alignment of your desire. As you progress through the day, your vibration may be skewed by your experiences. But this interruption doesn't take hold because, during the day, your vibration will be charged once more with the affirmation as you write it out. Before going to sleep, your affirmation is the last thing on your mind, which will charge your subconscious throughout the night. When we sleep, our beliefs are written into our subconscious, and with your affirmation taking root in your subconscious, you are more likely to rewrite your limiting beliefs and replace them with the power of your affirmation.

The 369 scripting method is practiced for at least 33 days and up to 45 days, but if your desire manifests before the time is up, you can close the practice with a gratitude meditation. For many people, the manifestation unfolds around the 21st day.

However, this doesn't mean you should quit if you don't get your manifestation by then. As with everything related to manifesting, patience is key. The universe works in its time, which is always the right time.

There are more scripting techniques you can choose to indulge in, especially if you have an angel number you'd like to manifest in your physical reality. When I needed an emotional breakthrough, I tried the 99x9 method, which helped me smash through the blocks that were stopping my emotional expressions. You can also use the specific angel numbers you need to manifest a specific reality. For example, if you need a change in your life, 11x11 combined with an affirmation calling for change is a great way to align your vibration with a new path. You can also choose to use a courage affirmation with the 11x11 scripting method to overcome your fear of the unknown. The possibilities are endless, so lean into your intuition and Divine Guidance to show you the way.

As we close this chapter, I'd like to mention a few rituals you can add to your scripting time to boost the power of your affirmations and vibrational alignment. You are not required to indulge in these activities, but if they seem interesting to you, please don't hesitate to try them.

Scripting and Moon Magic

The lunar cycle is a great manifestation tool because of the symbolism of each moon phase. If your desire is not urgent, and you can remain patient for a few days - depending on the present moon phase - you can include the moon's energy in your manifestation journey. The new moon, when the sun's yang and moon's yin energy are in perfect alignment, is a symbol of new beginnings. Because of this, the new moon is a perfect time to start your manifestation journey. By starting your scripting, whichever technique you choose, during the new moon, you are tapping into the moon's power also, allowing its energy to fuel your intentions. As the waxing lunar phases unfold, focus on your intentions, adding power to them through visualization, affirmations (if your scripting is done), inspired action, and gratitude meditation.

The full moon marks the start of the waning phases, the perfect time to reflect on your set intention, bring it to focus, and see how far you've come. Then, reflect on what is holding you back, and what is in the way of your manifestation. The full moon's appearance marks the perfect time for clearing and cleansing, and this is the time to let go of what is holding you back. As the waning phases unfold, deep dive into yourself. Introspect and reflect, understanding where you are, who you are, and what beliefs are stopping your manifestation. Connect with your

Divine intuition, and embrace its guidance. With the appearance of the waxing crescent moon, reflect on your desires, lessons, and intentions. Review the changes that have unfolded throughout the lunar cycle. Has your desire manifested? Even if the answer to this question is "no," there are still aspects of the desire that have come to fruition. Don't give up. Instead, embark on your manifestation when the new moon appears. You are starting from a position of abundance, not lack, and every time you charge your intention, your vibration grows.

Scripting and Candle Magic

Fire is a powerful element, and adding a candle to your scripting time is a great way to find a point of focus whenever your mind starts drifting from your page. While you may believe that you can write the same lines over and over again without losing focus, the reality is marginally different. No matter how good we are at focusing, the monotonous nature of scripting means that our minds are bound to drift even as we perform the task at hand. I usually have a problem reining in my mind when it starts drifting, so I added a candle to the scripting ritual. Whenever I catch myself drifting, I stare at the flame for a few moments, and I write slower to ensure my mind reads the words on the paper. I usually buy colored tealight candles.

Technically, my candle scripting ritual not only involves the power of the flame, but also the symbolic power of color. I light a different color depending on my intention, and sometimes I have two colors lit, usually white and a second color. For me, white is the symbol of my mind's purity and the clarity of my intention, no matter what it is. I also use a white candle when meditating as it reminds me of my ultimate goal - clarity in my physical, emotional, psychological, and spiritual journey. By incorporating the candle's color into your scripting, you boost your intention, adding the power of the color to your vibration. For example, lighting a green candle for an abundance intention is an exceptional choice because green is associated with abundance. Pink is associated with love, both romantic and platonic love. However, remember that pink is for the stable kind of love. Red, however, is the color of passion and lust. You can light both pink and red candles if your intention is to spark passion back into your relationship.

Let's explore a few candle colors and their meanings;

- **White**: serenity, purity, peace, personal strength.
- **Black**: protection, especially psychic.
- **Green**: prosperity, abundance, financial success.
- **Blue**: harmony, calm, emotional peace, tranquility.
- **Yellow**: communication, focus, knowledge, intellect.

- **Red**: passion, lust, sex, vitality, power, explosive energy.

- **Pink**: romance, joy, affection, self-love, friendship, compassion, warmth, faith.

- **Purple**: wisdom, spiritual enlightenment, spiritual awareness.

- **Orange**: creation, ambition, vibrant energy.

- **Brown**: fertility, growth, comfort, stability, resources.

- **Silver/Gray**: goddess (yin) energy, neutrality, banishing negative energy, stability.

- **Gold:** high vibration, wealth, great fortune.

Scripting and Color Magic

Incorporating color into your scripting is a fun way to boost your vibrational alignment, and there are myriad ways you can do this. You can use a pen with a color corresponding to your intention, or wear clothing matching the desired intention. Even something as small as an accessory can be a great vibrational booster, so have fun with it.

We've already explored the colors and their interpretations, so feel free to use the same interpretations to direct your choices.

To focus your intention and identify the item as a manifestation companion, charge it by blessing it before you start scripting. This way, you dedicate the color's power to your manifestation.

Manifesting is a fun and engaging process that calls for your dedication and faith in the universe. If you can add more flare to the practice to raise your vibration, it is welcome. The process of co-creating with the universe is meant to be a fulfilling experience. By adding angel number manifestations and other complimentary rituals, you set yourself up to make the most of your experience. If you are skeptical about the rituals, don't force yourself to indulge, as this will be counterproductive to your manifestation. The goal is to boost your vibrational alignment, not skew it.

Takeaway

In this chapter, we've explored:

- Setting yourself up for scripting

- Scripting techniques - 222, 444, 555, 777, and 369 manifestation methods

- Complementary scripting rituals - moon magic, candle magic, and color magic

Conclusion

We've come a long way from the beginning of this book, and we've explored the world of angel numbers through its numerology roots to its modern application. Angel numbers are a wonderful manifestation experience, as they are the sign you have been waiting for. Manifestation is a journey that is rarely straightforward, and it's easy to feel like nothing is happening. The Law of Attraction calls for patience in manifesting, but we are human, and patience can sometimes be hard to embody, especially when faced with unprecedented challenges as we pursue our desires. Angel numbers make this journey a little less lonely, as they give us something to look forward to.

When angel numbers appear, we are comforted by the presence of Divine Source. We are reminded that we are not alone and never will be, even if we may be tempted to forget that. Angel numbers show us the path to our true selves through our

Destiny and Life Path Numbers. We are pushed to strive for authenticity, to embrace who we are if we want to live the life we desire, the life we are called to live. Even when we don't see angel numbers, they help us connect to Divine Source through our alignment practices. Interpreting angel numbers also connects us to Divine Source, drawing us into ourselves to find out the messages we are receiving.

The Magic of Angel Numbers is in the way it complements every aspect of our manifestation journey, offering guidance, pushing us to alignment, focusing our intentions, and alerting us to our manifested desires. So, as you embark on your journey through the phases of manifesting, lean on your guardian angels, and call for their help through angel numbers. This way, you'll rejoice in the divine connection between you and the universe through your manifestation journey.

Thank You

"Happiness springs from doing good and helping others."
— Plato

Those who help others without any expectations in return experience more fulfillment, have higher levels of success, and live longer.

I want to create the opportunity for you to do this during this reading experience. For this, I have a very simple question... If it didn't cost you money, would you help someone you've never met before, even if you never got credit for it? If so, I want to ask for a favor on behalf of someone you do not know and likely never will. They are just like you and me, or perhaps how you were a few years ago...Less experienced, filled with the desire to help the world, seeking good information but not sure where to look…this is where you can help. The only way for us at Dreamlifepress to accomplish our mission of helping people on their spiritual growth journey is to first, reach them. And most people do judge a book by its reviews. So, if you have found this book helpful, would you please take a quick moment right now to leave an honest review of the book? It will cost you nothing and less than 60 seconds. Your review will help a stranger find this book and benefit from it.

One more person finds peace and happiness…one more person may find their passion in life…one more person experience a transformation that otherwise would never have happened…To make that come true, all you have to do is to leave a review. If you're on audible, click on the three dots in the top right of your screen, rate and review. If you're reading on a e-reader or kindle, just scroll to the bottom of the book, then swipe up and it will ask for a review. If this doesn't work, you can go to the book page on amazon or wherever store you purchased this from and leave a review from that page.

PS - If you feel good about helping an unknown person, you are my kind of people. I'm excited to continue helping you in your spiritual growth journey.

PPS - A little life hack - if you introduce something valuable to

Thank You

someone, they naturally associate that value to you. If you think this book can benefit anyone you know, send this book their way and build goodwill. From the bottom of my heart, thank you.

Your biggest fan – **Layla**

References

5 Powerful Ways To Manifest With Angel Numbers (Rituals). (2022, May 24). Manifest Like Whoa! https://manifestlikewhoa.com/manifest-with-angel-numbers/

Astrotalk. (n.d.). *Kabbalah Numerology: Components, Prediction Method & Importance*. Retrieved October 24, 2022, from https://astrotalk.com/numerology-introduction/kabbalah

Balliett, L. Dow. (1920). How to attain success through the strength of vibration of numbers: a system of numbers as taught by Pythagoras. 8th ed. Atlantic City, NJ: The author; etc., etc..

Chaldean Numerology - The numerology chart numbers. (n.d.). Numerology Toolbox. Retrieved October 24, 2022, from https://numerologytoolbox.com/numerology/chaldean-numerology/

Chaldean Numerology for Beginners: How Your Name and Birthday Reveal Your True Nature & Life Path - Kindle edition by Lagan, Heather Alicia. Religion & Spirituality Kindle eBooks @ Amazon.com. (n.d.). Retrieved October 24, 2022

References

Coughlin, S. (2022, March 24). *Your Life Path Number Is More Than A Personality Type*. Refinery29. https://www.refinery29.com/en-us/life-path-number-numerology-meaning

Estrada, J. (2022, October 13). *Laws of the Universe: Practice the 12 Laws of Nature & Improve Your Life*. Well+Good. https://www.wellandgood.com/laws-of-the-universe/

Hurst, K. (2021, September 20). *The 12 Spiritual Laws Of The Universe And What They Mean*. The Law of Attraction. https://thelawofattraction.com/12-spiritual-laws-universe/

Kelly, A. (2021, December 1). *A Beginner's Guide to Numerology: How to Find Your Life Path Number*. Allure. https://www.allure.com/story/numerology-how-to-calculate-life-path-destiny-number

Lauretta, A. (2022, October 22). *What are Angel Numbers? Numerology Meanings of Angel Numbers*. Parade: Entertainment, Recipes, Health, Life, Holidays. https://parade.com/1158156/ashleylauretta/what-are-angel-numbers/

Magazine, B. (2022, April 29). *What Are Angel Numbers? A Brief History*. Brazzil. https://www.brazzil.com/what-are-angel-numbers-a-brief-history/

Moon Rituals: How To Manifest With The Moon. (2021, May 7). Jennifer Racioppi. https://jenniferracioppi.com/moon-rituals-how-to-manifest-with-the-moon/

Numerology: Your Life Path Number, Angel Numbers and More | Astrostyle: Astrology and Daily, Weekly, Monthly. (2022, August 20). Astrostyle:

Astrology and Daily, Weekly, Monthly Horoscopes by the AstroTwins. https://astrostyle.com/numerology/

Tamil Numerology Numbers: Find your Destiny Number. (2021, November 13). MyPandit. https://www.mypandit.com/numerology/tamil-numerology/

Team, E. U. (2020, December 31). *Different Types Of Angel Numbers: A Quick Guide.* EnlightenmentU. https://enlightenmentu.com/different-types-of-angel-numbers/

The Ultimate Guide to Numerology. (2022, October 19). InStyle. https://www.instyle.com/lifestyle/astrology/numerology

Young, A. (2020, October 11). *Kabbalah Numerology - Come Discover What Your Life Path Number Is.* Subconscious Servant. https://subconsciousservant.com/kabbalah-numerology/

Printed in Great Britain
by Amazon